T0358232

The World Bank and
Social Transformation in
International Politics

In the 1990s the World Bank changed its policy and took the position that the problems of poverty and governance are inextricably linked. Improving the governance of its borrower countries became progressively accepted as a legitimate part of the World Bank's development activities. This book examines why the World Bank came to see good governance as important, and evaluates what the World Bank is doing to improve the governance of its borrower countries.

David Williams examines changing World Bank policy since the late 1970s to show how a concern with good governance grew out of the problems it experienced over structural adjustment lending, particularly in sub-Saharan Africa. Whilst providing an account of the early years of the World Bank through the to 1990s, the book also systematically relates the policies of good governance to liberalism. A detailed case study of World Bank lending to Ghana demonstrates what the attempt to improve 'governance' looks like in practice. Williams assesses whether the World Bank has been successful in its attempts to improve governance, and draws out some of the implications of the argument for how we should think about sovereignty and how we should understand the connections between liberalism and international politics.

This book will be of interest to students and scholars of international relations, politics, economics, development and African studies.

David Williams is Lecturer at the Centre for International Politics, City University, UK. His research interests are in the area of international relations of development. He has previously published in *Political Studies*, *Review of International Studies* and *Millennium*.

Routledge/Warwick Studies in Globalisation

Edited by Richard Higgott and published in association with the Centre for the Study of Globalisation and Regionalisation, University of Warwick.

What is globalisation and does it matter? How can we measure it? What are its policy implications? The Centre for the Study of Globalisation and Regionalisation at the University of Warwick is an international site for the study of key questions such as these in the theory and practice of globalisation and regionalisation. Its agenda is avowedly interdisciplinary. The work of the Centre will be showcased in this series. This series comprises two strands:

Warwick Studies in Globalisation addresses the needs of students and teachers, and the titles will be published in hardback and paperback. Titles include:

Globalisation and the Asia-Pacific
Contested territories
Edited by Kris Olds, Peter Dicken, Philip F. Kelly, Lily Kong and Henry Wai-chung Yeung

Regulating the Global Information Society
Edited by Christopher Marsden

Banking on Knowledge
The genesis of the global development network
Edited by Diane Stone

Historical Materialism and Globalisation
Edited by Hazel Smith and Mark Rupert

Civil Society and Global Finance
Edited by Jan Aart Scholte with Albrecht Schnabel

Towards a Global Polity
Edited by Morten Ougaard and Richard Higgott

New Regionalisms in the Global Political Economy
Theories and cases
Edited by Shaun Breslin, Christopher W. Hughes, Nicola Phillips and Ben Rosamond

Development Issues in Global Governance
Public–private partnerships and market multilateralism
Benedicte Bull and Desmond McNeill

Globalizing Democracy
Political parties in emerging democracies
Edited by Peter Burnell

The Globalization of Political Violence
Globalization's shadow
Edited by Richard Devetak and Christopher W. Hughes

Regionalisation and Global Governance
The taming of globalisation?
Edited by Andrew F. Cooper, Christopher W. Hughes and Philippe De Lombaerde

Routledge/Warwick Studies in Globalisation is a forum for innovative new research intended for a high-level specialist readership, and the titles will be available in hardback only. Titles include:

1. Non-State Actors and Authority in the Global System
Edited by Richard Higgott, Geoffrey Underhill and Andreas Bieler

2. Globalisation and Enlargement of the European Union
Austrian and Swedish social forces in the struggle over membership
Andreas Bieler

3. Rethinking Empowerment
Gender and development in a global/local world
Edited by Jane L. Parpart, Shirin M. Rai and Kathleen Staudt

4. Globalising Intellectual Property Rights
The TRIPs agreement
Duncan Matthews

5. Globalisation, Domestic Politics and Regionalism
The ASEAN Free Trade Area
Helen E. S. Nesadurai

6. Microregionalism and Governance in East Asia
Katsuhiro Sasuga

The World Bank and Social Transformation in International Politics

Liberalism, governance and sovereignty

David Williams

Routledge
Taylor & Francis Group

LONDON AND NEW YORK

First published 2008 by Routledge
2 Park Square, Milton Park, Abingdon, Oxon, OX14 4RN

Simultaneously published in the USA and Canada
by Routledge
605 Third Avenue, New York, NY 10017

Routledge is an imprint of the Taylor & Francis Group, an informa business

Typeset in Times New Roman by
Bookcraft Limited, Stroud, Gloucestershire

British Library Cataloguing in Publication Data
A catalogue record for this book is available from the British
Library

Library of Congress Cataloging in Publication Data
Williams, David, 1969–
The World Bank and social transformation in international
politics : liberalism, governance and sovereignty / David
Williams.
p. cm. – (Routledge/Warwick studies in globalisation)
Includes bibliographical references and index.
1. World Bank. 2. Liberalism. 3. Public administration.
I. Title.
HG3881.5.W57W53 2008
332.1'532–dc22   2007040182

ISBN13: 978-0-415-45300-4 (hbk)
ISBN13: 978-0-415-66414-1 (pbk)
ISBN13: 978-0-203-92879-0 (ebk)

Publisher's Note
The publisher has gone to great lengths to ensure the quality of this reprint
but points out that some imperfections in the original may be apparent.

Contents

Acknowledgements

I have incurred many, many debts during the long and tortuous process of writing this book. I started working on the World Bank as a graduate student in the Department of Political Studies at SOAS. I am very grateful to the ESRC for providing financial assistance during this time. The department was a particularly stimulating and supportive place to work. In particular I would like to thank Katherine Dean, John Game, Richard Jeffries, Sudipta Kaviraj, and Donal Cruise O'Brien. Toby Dodge and Nick Hostettler have remained close friends since that time and have provided support and encouragement over the many years since we first met. Toby in particular deserves a big thank you for helping me over a difficult time. After SOAS I was lucky enough to be appointed as Hedley Bull and Talbot Junior Research Fellow at Lady Margaret Hall Oxford. LMH was a lovely place to work, and particular thanks go to Gillian Peele, Frances Lannon and Gregor Irwin. After LMH I moved to the Department of Politics and International Relations at Oxford, where I owe particular debts to Neil MacFarlane and Adam Roberts. Adam offered a very sage piece of advice about the book which took a long time to sink in, and Neil provided support and encouragement during the whole time I was at Oxford. The final manuscript was prepared while in the nascent centre for International Politics at City University, London. Thanks there to John Solomos and Tony Woodiwiss. Charles Kenny deserves a special mention for everything he has done over the years. My greatest intellectual debt is to Tom Young. He was my PhD supervisor and we have worked together on the issues this book tries to tackle since then. He has been a constant source of encouragement, criticism and intellectual stimulation. This book is dedicated to Tanya Epstein. I could not have finished it without her love and support.

Introduction

In a report published in 1989 the World Bank first publicly indicated its commitment to the idea that 'good governance' was important for development success (World Bank 1989). Given how ubiquitous the idea of good governance has become in development circles, it is easy to forget how controversial this was at the time. In particular, the idea of good governance seemed to signal that the Bank was taking 'politics' more seriously – something that many people inside and outside the Bank were opposed to. Through the 1990s, however, improving the governance of its borrower countries became increasingly accepted as a legitimate and important part of the World Bank's development activities. Indeed, the World Bank now argues that 'the problems of poverty and governance are inextricably linked', and that 'strengthening governance is an essential precondition for improving the lives of the poor' (World Bank 2002a: 271). This book considers two questions: why the World Bank came to see 'good governance' as important, and what the World Bank is doing to improve the 'governance' of its borrower countries.

Part of the answer to these questions is provided by an empirical account of policy change and implementation. The book examines changing World Bank policy since the late 1970s to show how a concern with good governance grew out of the problems the World Bank was experiencing with structural adjustment lending, particularly in sub-Saharan Africa. The book also examines in some detail World Bank lending to Ghana to show what the attempt to improve 'governance' looks like in practice. What this book insists on, however, is that the process of policy change and implementation can only be understood by reference to the ideas about social transformation that underpin the policies and practice of good governance. This book argues that good governance is a specifically liberal project of social transformation.[1] What drives this argument is the view that liberalism is more than simply a body of normative political theory about, for example, such issues as political obligation or justice. Rather, liberalism is a way of thinking about social transformation. While this is an unusual way of thinking about liberal thought, it really should not be; after all, historically liberal thinkers were concerned, perhaps above all, with changing the world around them.

Liberalism, understood as a project of social transformation, then, is in international politics in the sense that it is expressed through the policies and practices of the World Bank. This is a rather different view of the connections between liberalism and international politics than those dominant within the discipline of International Relations. A very great deal has been written about the relationship between liberalism and international relations. Much of this literature has remained at the level of normative political theory, and has produced extensive debates about such things as the nature of international obligations, redistributive justice and human rights. Much less attention has been paid to how, exactly, liberals have tried to make their commitments real in the world. Partly this is because many within the discipline of International Relations have presumed that such attempts are likely to prove fruitless. Nonetheless, some of this work is emerging, focusing for example, on the role of NGOs, international organizations, and campaigning groups in changing state behaviour (Finnemore 1996; Keck and Sikkink 1998). Very little attention, however, has been paid to the kinds of strategies, tactics and techniques employed by organizations devoted to the task of making liberalism real in the politics, economies and societies of developing countries. And this is exactly what the World Bank is trying to do. To substantiate this argument it is necessary to examine both World Bank policy and the details of its lending practices. The examination of Bank policy reveals how it replicates characteristic liberal positions on the state, the economy, civil society and the individual. The examination of its lending practices brings to the fore the connections between the techniques and strategies employed in its development projects and liberal thought about the possibilities of social transformation.

Examining the policies and practices of good governance also reveals the extent to which the sovereignty of many developing countries has been severely compromised. The World Bank's pursuit of 'good governance' signals the end of what we might call the 'sovereignty regime' that shaped the external relations of many of these countries up to the end of the Cold War. The sovereignty accorded to many post-colonial states was historically unusual, as Robert Jackson has argued (Jackson 1993). But there existed a general commitment to the idea that these states were sovereign, and that their sovereignty was, in principal, desirable, both for them and for the conduct of international affairs. This in turn conditioned relations between these states and development agencies like the World Bank. Governments were understood to be the lead agent in the development project, and agencies like the World Bank generally limited themselves to the provision of capital and technical assistance. In contrast, the pursuit of 'good governance' entails detailed and highly intrusive development interventions in almost all aspects of social, political, and economic life. The rise of a concern with governance signals then not just the significance of liberalism in international politics, but also the declining significance of sovereignty as a way of organizing relations between developed and less developed states.

Liberalism and the World Bank

Arguing that the World Bank's pursuit of good governance is a liberal project of social transformation requires making two initial analytical steps. The first is to argue that 'ideas' matter for explaining what the World Bank does, and the second is to argue that the relevant ideas are best described as 'liberal' rather than 'neo-liberal' – a term more often used in descriptions of World Bank policy.

There is a great deal of literature which suggests that what the World Bank does can be explained without reference to ideas. It comes in essentially two forms. First, there is the argument that the World Bank is controlled or substantially influenced by its major shareholders, particularly the United States, and thus that the Bank is essentially an instrument of US foreign policy, or at least the foreign policies of Western states. It has been argued, for example, that 'without any doubt' the World Bank is a 'political arm of the big industrial governments, mainly the United States', and that the activities of the World Bank 'must be of such a nature to reflect primarily US economic, financial and political interests', or that it is 'dominated by the interests and politics of the rich', which include the US, Britain, Germany, France, and Japan (Feder 1976: 334; George 1976: 263). Again, it has been suggested that the Bank is 'necessarily biased towards the interests of its major shareholders', that it has 'been obedient to the wishes of the US executive branch ever since it was founded', and that the US 'has always been able to control the direction of its lending' (Hayter and Watson 1985: 150; see also Payer 1982).

A second line of analysis has been concerned with showing that the interests of the World Bank itself, or of its component bureaucratic parts, are central to explaining what it does (Vaudel 1991). Philippe Le Pestre, for example, has argued that the World Bank, like all international organizations, has three 'fundamental goals': survival, decision-making autonomy and control over resources; all of which take precedence over the pursuit of the purposes for which it was created (Le Pestre 1986; see also Burnham 1994). Barbara Crane and Jason Finkle analyzed the emergence and practice of the World Bank's population control programmes during the 1970s

(Crane and Finkle 1981). While the need for such programmes was accepted by Western governments, it was not accepted by many Bank staff. Crane and Finkle argued that the programmes 'lacked a strong base in the internal organizational structure of the bank' and were hence subordinated to other priorities. They argued that the implementation of these programmes was shaped by the special relationship that staff members developed with their clients, particularly ministries of finance, which they were unwilling to jeopardize by giving population control a high priority (Crane and Finkle 1981: 518; see also Ascher 1983).

Neither of these two arguments is wholly wrong. There is indeed plenty of evidence that the US government has influenced aspects of the Bank's operations and policies (Gwin 1997). There is good evidence that the Bank was pressured by the US to suspend lending to Chile after Allende's election in 1970, to Vietnam in 1977, Nicaragua in the 1980s and Iran in the 1980s and 1990s (Brown 1992: 157–70, 185–90; See also Kapur 2002). There is also evidence of a direct attempt by the Reagan administration to pressure the Bank into adopting a more 'market friendly' approach to development (Ayres 1983: 230–2). In recent years Robert Wade has traced the influence of the US government, and particularly the US treasury, in a series of articles. He has argued that 'American values and interests' are of 'determining importance' in the functioning of the Bank (Wade 1996: 35). More concretely he has argued that the high-profile departure of then Chief Economist Joseph Stiglitz from the Bank in 1999 was the result of direct pressure from the US Treasury (Wade 2001). One obvious factor identified as a source of control over the World Bank is voting power on the Board of Directors. In general the amount of votes a country has on the Board is determined by the amount of capital that countries pay into the Bank, and this means that voting power is heavily concentrated in Executive Directors which represent Western governments.[2] The US currently holds the largest share of the votes, about 17 per cent, followed by Japan with about 6 per cent, and Germany, France and Britain, each with around 5 per cent. The Board is charged with the day-to-day running of the Bank, and approves all loans, policies, and Bank reports. There are also more 'informal' mechanisms for the US to exercise influence. One commentator has suggested that 'any signal of displeasure by the US executive director has an almost palpable impact on the Bank leadership and staff' (Ascher 1992: 124).

The stress on the bureaucratic nature of the World Bank also reveals something significant about it as an institution. It is a large, complex and diverse organization. There are more than 8,000 staff working in over 60 separate departments in Washington, DC, and more than 65 field offices. Staff specializations range from macroeconomic modelling to marine conservation and from decentralization to debt management. In an organization such as this there are going to be disputes and disagreements and problems of communication and coordination. These problems have led to periodic attempts to reorganize the Bank in order to make it more efficient and 'results focused'; although it is doubtful if these reorganizations have overcome the almost inevitable bureaucratic problems associated with organizations of this size (Weaver and Leiteritz 2005). It is also the case that the World Bank's mission has expanded remarkably in the last twenty years, and this book is partly about that expansion.

What the World Bank does, however, cannot be reduced simply to these two elements. In recent years there has emerged a consensus that in fact the World Bank is relatively autonomous from its major shareholders.[3] First, despite the formal and informal power of the US, the Bank's top management has in fact shown a remarkable ability to resist pressure from the Executive Board, in large part because of the time pressures facing Board members, their relative lack of expertise, and the sheer size and complexity of the Bank (Vetterlein 2007: 133–4). Second, much of the World Bank's more routine work is not of direct political and economic significance to the major states; this is certainly the case with many of the projects reviewed in this book. It is simply wrong to draw a direct line between the interests of the US government and a water and sanitation project in Ghana. Or, to put it anther way, we should make a distinction between this kind of routine everyday Bank activity and the Bank's response to certain crises (for example the East Asian Financial Crisis) or its activities in certain politically strategic states, where the influence of its major shareholders is likely to be more significant (Woods 2006). This is not to deny the influence of the US on many aspects of the Bank's functioning and operations, it simply means that what the Bank does cannot be explained solely with reference to the actions and interests of the US. The bureaucratic nature of the World Bank is important, particularly for the process of policy change within the Bank. Indeed if it is the case that the World Bank has some autonomy from its major shareholders then some attempt to get inside the 'black box' of the Bank is likely to be important if we want to explain how and why the World Bank's policies and practices change over time (Vetterlein 2007; Gulrajani 2007).

What both of these views are missing, however, is any account of how the World Bank has come to think about development; an account, that is, of how it thinks about and conceives of the problems facing developing countries, and how it thinks about and conceives of solutions to these problems. We want to know, in other words, what the World Bank's 'collective image' of development is.[4] The argument of this book is that it is liberalism which provides the Bank with the resources for thinking about development.

This stress on liberalism is in some contrast to the term 'neo-liberalism' that is more often used to describe the World Bank's development policies. As a description of World Bank policies, 'neo-liberalism' came to the fore in the 1980s, as the World Bank came to stress market liberalization and marketization through its structural adjustment programmes. Used in this way 'neo-liberal' was synonymous with the resurgence of 'neo-classical' economics in development policy (Toye 1987). There is a certain merit to the term 'neo-liberal' as a description of Bank policy in the 1980s, but it is too narrow a term to describe Bank policy in the 1990s and particularly the ideas of good governance. It is not that the World Bank has moved away from a commitment to the allocative efficiency of the market mechanism; it is rather that the Bank has come to embrace a much broader account of social transformation that includes, but goes much beyond, the establishment of markets. Even those who continue to embrace the term neo-liberalism have recognized that the emergence of good governance signals a much wider development project. Craig and Porter, for example, argue that changes in development policy since the 1990s can be cast as the political and economic project of a 'wider historical liberalism' (Craig and Porter 2006: 7). They still want to hang on to the term 'neoliberalism' but to append to it the labels 'inclusive' or 'positive' to distinguish it from the 'conservative' neoliberalism that, so they argue, characterized the era of structural adjustment (Craig and Porter 2006: 21). Similarly, Graham Harrison has argued that the policies of the World Bank are best seen as 'neoliberal', but that in their more recent phase they indicate a desire to 'embed' liberalism that requires going beyond the 'neoliberal fundamentals' to include the engineering of states and societies (Harrison 2004: 66).

While there is much to agree with in Craig and Porter's and Harrison's accounts of the World Bank and good governance, the utility of hanging on to the 'neoliberal' label is unclear, especially as what the World Bank is doing goes far beyond 'market fundamentals'. Second, the project of radical social transformation that they see in 'neoliberalism' is not very different in kind from other versions of the liberal project. That is, neoliberalism is not a special or unusual kind of liberalism, it is liberalism. Finally, and related, the use of the term 'neoliberalism' lets liberalism 'off the hook' as it were, by implying there is some other kind of liberalism that does not imply or require the transformation of social institutions and practices. As will become clear in the next chapter, liberalism in its entirety has been fundamentally concerned with social transformation.

This book argues then, that the policies and practices of 'good governance' are a specifically liberal project of social transformation. Liberalism provides the concepts, categories and arguments of the policies of good governance, and the content of World Bank projects and programmes derives from its commitment to liberalism. Finally, the process of policy change within the World Bank has been structured by a set of commitments to liberalism. This process of policy change has involved other elements too, including at various times the influence of Western states, and certain bureaucratic features of the Bank as an organization. Nonetheless, the central process has been a working through of the implications of the concepts and categories of liberal thought for development policy and practice.

The normative question

If it is right that the World Bank is engaged in a liberal project of social transformation, what are we to make of it? It might be argued, and many liberals would argue, that this is highly desirable. To the extent that the World Bank succeeds in its project, they might say, then all to the good. This argument can be made in two ways. One can simply argue that liberalism provides the 'right' way for societies to be organized, or one can argue that the achievement of liberal institutions and practices is highly functional in the modern world in that it allows countries to benefit from profitable engagement with the international economy and so achieve growth and development. Both ways of responding suggest that the erosion of sovereignty that has accompanied the rise of good governance is an entirely acceptable price to pay for the achievement of liberalism.

An initial response to these kinds of arguments is to say that discussions about what Western agencies should and should not be doing ought to be conducted on the basis of what they are actually doing. Far too often the self-descriptions produced by these agencies are taken as the basis for an assessment of whether their activities should be supported. What this book suggests is that we withhold judgement until we have a better sense of what is actually entailed in the introduction of liberal institutions and practices. When we do have a better sense of this we might start to feel rather less comfortable about unquestionably endorsing these activities. 'Good governance' entails a detailed reworking of the way people conceive of themselves and their social relations, and a deliberate and fine-grained attempt to eliminate certain ways of being. This project is currently being pursued by external agencies that purport to have privileged access to knowledge about how societies should be organized. And all of this is taking place with no guarantee of success. We may still decide that on balance it is desirable for the World Bank to be pursuing this project of social transformation. But we should at least be aware of what this entails before we draw that conclusion.

Outline

The next chapter tries to substantiate the claim that liberalism can be understood as a project of social transformation. The key conceptual shift here is to have an expanded account of what liberalism can be. Too often liberalism is taken simply to be a body of normative theorizing. We suggest instead, that liberalism be understood as a project of social transformation, and that liberal theorizing should be understood as an extended reflection on the desirability and possibility of this transformation. Chapter two examines the foundation and early years of the World Bank, but it does so by examining aspects of the normative structure of international politics, and the emergence and institutionalization of the idea of 'development'. Chapter three traces the emergence of a concern with good governance since the late 1970s, stressing in particular how the World Bank responded to the problems and failures of structural adjustment lending. Chapter four looks at the increasing acceptance of the idea of good governance within the Bank through the 1990s, and then systematically relates the policies of good governance to liberalism. Chapter five looks at how the World Bank has attempted to improve governance in Ghana. Finally, chapter six makes an initial assessment of how successful or otherwise the World Bank has been in its attempts to improve governance, and draws out some of the implications of the argument for how we should think about sovereignty, for how we should understand the connections between liberalism and international politics, and for the normative question we posed above.

1 Liberalism and social transformation

This chapter argues that liberalism can be understood as a project of social transformation. It begins by clarifying the kinds of arguments typically had about what liberalism is. Characteristically, an answer to the question of what liberalism is focuses on this or that element of liberal normative theory – rights, freedom, equality and so on. The problem with this view is that liberal normative theory is diverse and in some respects contradictory, thus making it difficult to come to any agreement about what is 'really' or properly liberal. An alternative is to recast the debate by arguing that liberalism is not simply, or even largely, normative political theory. Barry Hindess, for example, has proposed the liberalism be understood as a 'project of government'. We follow Hindess in suggesting that liberalism is more than normative theory, and we also agree with Hindess that having such an expanded account of liberalism helps make sense of some of the tensions and ambiguities within liberal normative theory. We depart from Hindess in suggesting that liberalism is a project of social transformation and not simply a project of government (although we think that Hindess is correct in identifying the problem of government as a significant element of liberal thought). The rest of the chapter is concerned with substantiating the account of liberalism as a project of social transformation through an examination of liberal thought. That is, we remain for the time being on the terrain of theory, but we try to show that liberal theory has been substantially concerned with social transformation.

Debating liberalism

The traditional approach to the question, 'What is liberalism?' has been to concentrate on the concepts and arguments found in the classical texts of liberal thought. Some thinkers have attempted to search for a 'core' idea which characterizes liberalism in general. Jeremy Waldron, for example, has argued that all liberal thinking is characterized by a commitment 'to a conception of freedom and of respect for the capacities and the agency of individual men and women, and that these commitments generate a requirement that all aspects of the social world either be made acceptable, or be capable of being made acceptable to every last individual' (Waldron 1987: 128, 135). In a similar vein Stanley Hoffman, in his famous article 'Liberalism and International Affairs', defined liberalism as 'the doctrine whose central concern is the liberty of the individual' (Hoffman 1986: 395). Richard Dworkin, by contrast, has argued that a 'certain conception of *equality* ... is the nerve of liberalism'. This conception of equality, he argues, is that the government must treat all its citizens equally in regard to their own conceptions of the good (Dworkin 1985a: 183, 190–1). The disagreement between these accounts of liberalism (one stressing liberty, the other a certain kind of equality) suggests that defining liberalism through its core concepts is very difficult. This has led some thinkers to suggest that there is really no such thing as 'liberalism' at all. Arthur O. Lovejoy argued that, 'the doctrines or tendencies that are designated by familiar names ending in *-ism* ... [are] compounds ... [A]ll these trouble-breeding and usually thought-obscuring terms ... are names of complexes not of simples ... They stand as a rule not for one doctrine, but for several distinct and often conflicting doctrines' (Lovejoy 1936: 5-6). In a similar vein, John Dunn has said that 'liberalism is a term of extreme imprecision of reference', and John Gray, that 'liberalism' has 'no unchanging nature or essence' (Dunn 1979: 29; J. Gray 1986: ix).

Despite their disagreements, participants in this debate remain committed to the view that arguments about what liberalism is, are arguments about the content of liberal normative theory. But it is not clear that we should feel bound by this account of liberalism. Indeed, one could argue that this view of liberalism is anachronistic in the sense that thinkers in the classical cannon of liberal thought were not simply, or even largely, engaged in *doing* normative political theory.[1] Given the dominance of a particular kind of analytical normative theory within the contemporary academic study of political theory, it is easy to reinterpret the arguments of these classical thinkers as normative theory. But the historical point of liberalism has been precisely its transformative or even revolutionary character, and many liberal thinkers were engaged substantially in intensely political arguments about social transformation. This is not to say that normative political theory is unimportant to liberalism; rather it is to say that we should recognise how much of this theorizing, at least historically, has been animated by broader political objectives.

One attempt to get beyond the idea of liberalism as normative political theory has been put forward by Barry Hindess (Hindess 2002a, 2002b, 2004). He argues that liberalism can be understood as a 'project of government'. By this he means that liberal thought has always been concerned with the problem of governing. Hindess uses the terms 'government' and 'government' here in ways derived from the work of Michel Foucault (Foucault 2001a, 2001b). Foucault drew attention to the emergence of a new concern with governing populations that emerged in eighteenth-century social thought. This concern arose, so Foucault suggested, as a result of the discovery of the 'social' and the 'market' as autonomous realms with their own internal dynamics. The problem of government was then the problem of how to govern (regulate, order and control) without disturbing the dynamics of these realms – particularly that of the market. What distinguished liberalism was its commitment to governing as far as possible through the promotion of certain kinds of free activity and the cultivation among the governed of suitable habits of self-regulation (Hindess 2004). Hindess expands and develops Foucault's account of liberalism as a 'rationality of government' in two important ways. First, Hindess is concerned to balance the books as it were, by drawing attention to the myriad ways in which liberal thinkers have advocated the use of coercion (rather than just regulated freedom) to govern. Second, and very importantly, Hindess locates the liberal desire to govern within the distinctions liberal thinkers have always made between the 'civilized' and 'uncivilized' or 'developed' and 'less developed' (Hindess 2002b). Thus for Hindess, a central part of liberalism has been its international or cosmopolitan vision, but this vision has been guided by a set of concepts that locate people and peoples on a spectrum – from uncivilized to civilized, less-developed to developed – that justifies the use of all kinds of coercive governmental techniques on those who cannot govern themselves.

Hindess puts forward two justifications for developing this account of liberalism (Hindess 2004). First, he argues that seeing liberalism as a project of government illuminates the actual practices of governing evident within liberal states (and within the attempts of these states to govern other places) (see also A. Barry *et al.* 1996). Second, he argues that seeing liberalism in this way provides a fuller and more powerful account of the work of central figures in the liberal tradition (Hindess 2004). There is a great deal to be gleaned from Hindess's account of liberalism. As this book proceeds certain similarities with his account of liberalism will become clear, especially the concern with the techniques and strategies of governing within liberal thought, and the stress on the cosmopolitan nature of liberal thought and practice. This book also follows Hindess's justifications for conceiving of liberalism as more than simply a body of normative political theory. It argues that the focus on liberalism as a project of social transformation helps illuminate the actual practices of the World Bank, and it argues that this conceptualization of liberalism makes better sense of some of the key thinkers within the liberal tradition, as well as helping to illuminate some of the key tensions and ambiguities within liberal thought.

In other words, thinking of liberalism as a project of social transformation helps connect political thought with political practice in illuminating ways, and helps make better sense of liberalism than the view that liberalism is a body of normative theory. Where we part company from Hindess is in the stress placed on the idea of social transformation rather than government. To be sure these are not contradictory views; the exercise of government is an essential part of the project of social transformation. Yet we place more emphasis on the 'kinetic' elements of liberalism; its restless and relentless desire to remake the world in its own image. It is this that ultimately underpins the liberal project. To pursue this argument we remain for the time being at the level of theory. But we treat liberal theory not simply as normative theory, but as an extended reflection on the desirability and possibility of social transformation.

The investigation proceeds in three stages. It is not too controversial to say that liberal theorizing has been overwhelmingly concerned with four spheres – the state, the economy, 'civil society' and the individual – and with the appropriate relationship between these spheres. Initially, we look at liberal theorizing about the state, the economy, and civil society. Obviously there is no space to undertake a detailed exposition of liberal thought in all these spheres; instead we identify some of the central tensions and ambiguities that characterize liberal thought about these spheres. We then move to the heart of liberal theorizing – its stress on the individual as the source of justification for liberal ends and as the central component of liberal theoretical strategies. But again here the concern is to show the typical ambivalence and ambiguity that characterizes liberal thought about persons. On the one hand, and in their more philosophical mode, liberal thinkers have tended to want to ground liberal thought in traits that are deemed 'natural' in one way or another: autonomy, the ability to reason, or 'the desire to truck, barter and exchange one thing for another' as Adam Smith put it. On the other hand, and in their more sociological mode, many of the same thinkers were profoundly impressed by how malleable people were – by how influenced they actually were by religion, custom and tradition; so much so that many of these supposedly 'natural' traits were absent from social life. Finally, we focus on those often neglected aspects of liberal thought that more obviously identify it as a political project. In particular, liberal thinkers advocated a series of techniques designed to change the way people thought and acted. These techniques rely on the fact that people are influenced by things like religion, custom and tradition. Thus, the promise of liberalism as liberation from various 'oppressive' institutions and practices is revealed to be insertion into new forms of discipline.

Liberal spheres and liberal ends

Considered as a stream of thinking, liberalism has been particularly concerned with four spheres: the state, the economy, civil society and the individual. This is not to say that the social world can adequately be divided up into these spheres, or that these liberal spheres represent a reasonably accurate picture of social life, either now or in the past. It might better be said that these spheres represents the world that liberal thinkers would like to see, rather than the one they actually do see. Obviously there is no space to undertake a detailed exposition of liberal thought in all these spheres; instead the object of this review is to identify some of the central tensions and ambiguities that characterize liberal thought about these spheres. Later, we suggest that these tensions and ambiguities can be understood in large part by seeing liberal theory as about social transformation.

The state

Liberals have very often been suspicious of the state. Yet, in almost all liberal thought, the state remains the central vehicle for the achievement of liberal ends and arrangements. The primary tension here then is that within liberal thought the state is conceived of as both weak and strong. The state must be weak because it is purely an enabler, little more than a neutral mechanism providing security to allow free, equal individuals to pursue their life projects unhindered by others. This view has been particularly prominent in contemporary liberal political theory (Goodin and Reeve 1989). It is most obviously associated with the work of John Rawls, and following Rawls, Richard Dworkin (Rawls 1971). According to Dworkin, the liberal state must be neutral on the question of the good life for individuals and thus political decisions must be, so far as possible, independent of any particular conception of the good (Dworkin 1985a). But it is quite clear that a strong strand of liberal thought, arguably from Hobbes and Locke onward, has justified the state on the basis that it is 'neutral' between competing conceptions of the good (Salkever 1990). Kant, for example, argued that a paternalistic government was the 'greatest conceivable despotism' as it imposes a particular morality and a particular view of what makes people happy (Kant 1970). In this view a strong state is a potential threat to free persons. First, the state may attempt to impose some particular social order, which will invariably embody some set of values that constrains people's freedom, and second, that the offices of the state may be abused by their incumbents (and the stronger the state the greater the possible abuses). Within liberal thought these threats are countered by the advocacy of a universal legal code to which state officials are also subject, the establishment of certain political rights, and the institutionalization of forms of political accountability (Paul, E. *et al.* 2005; Waldon 1984).

There is an extensive debate over exactly what the basis of the argument for a neutral state is, and liberals are characteristically ambivalent on this point (Galston 1982; Kymlicka 1989). On one hand liberals have appealed simply to the 'facts' of pluralism to demonstrate the desirability of a neutral state. As Locke says, 'men in this world prefer different things and pursue happiness by contrary courses' (Locke 1976: 123). In a related fashion, Rawls has suggested that neutrality is to be understood as a political not a metaphysical principle; the liberal state simply responds to the already existing pluralism in modern society (Rawls 1985, 1993a). On the other hand, liberals have very often relied on philosophical arguments, rather than political ones, to justify the neutral state, and in so doing have advanced conceptions of the good (Galston 1982; Sandel 1982). Hobbes and Locke both endorsed what would come to be called the 'bourgeois' goods of peace, comfort and security (Salkever 1990: 170). In doing so they endorsed these values as particularly appropriate for individuals. There is a good case for arguing that Rawls also has a particular conception of the good for persons at the heart of his theory (Sandel 1982). As Brian Barry has argued, 'there is no way in which non-liberals can be sold on the principle of neutrality without first injecting a large dose of liberalism into their outlook' (B. Barry 1990: 54). That is, arguments for the neutrality of the liberal state actually rest on substantive conceptions of the desirable way of life; or to put it another way, the neutrality principle applies between ways of life that are the expression of the choices of individuals already committed to the goods of liberalism (Galston 1982: 625).

This ambiguity about the grounding and extent of the neutrality principle points in the direction of the other vision of the state in liberal thought – that of the strong state. For while it might be right that all liberals think there should be domains of social life over which the state has no legitimate authority, they also want to see these domains created and sustained, and the only agency capable of doing that is the state. The strong state must to a certain extent be disengaged from social interests and certainly not overwhelmed by them; it must in other words, be 'autonomous' from society, at least up to a point, because it is only by being autonomous that the state is not prone to capture by social groups who would threaten the achievement of liberal ends. And this is where we should locate the anxiety that many liberal thinkers have had about the form and extent of democratic arrangements. This is especially clear, for example, in the work of John Stuart Mill (Mill 1972). This suggests that there is within liberalism a vision of the state as capable of imposing and maintaining a certain kind of social order – a liberal order. On this view it is quite impossible for the liberal state to be neutral and indifferent to values; rather, it must actively interfere in what people believe and how they live, even to the extent of inculcating certain kinds of values and dispositions. As Rawls put it, 'in agreeing to principles of right the parties in the original position consent to the arrangements necessary to make these principles affective in their conduct' (Rawls 1971: 515). Such elaborate processes of transformation of both institutions and practices require not a weak state, but rather a state constituted in the form of a bureaucratic apparatus with all the capacity for social surveillance and social control which that makes possible.

The tension between the idea of a weak state and the idea of a strong state is explicable in terms of the liberalism as a project of social transformation. To put it bluntly a strong state is necessary to construct and defend liberal institutions and practices, but once these are established and secure the state can afford to be 'neutral'. All of this might seem some way from the World Bank, but as we shall see, it is not. For these ambiguities about the state – weak but strong, neutral but partial, accountable but not captured – are exactly replicated in the way the World Bank thinks about the role of the state in development. And the central role that the state is understood to have in the liberal project is again exactly replicated in the World Bank's account of good governance.

The economy

The acceptance of the basic view that the economic realm has its own 'laws', and thus that it can be analyzed apart from other social spheres, has been the central claim of economic liberalism (Taylor 1990). This claim is most famously expressed in Adam Smith's metaphor of the 'invisible hand' (Ullmann-Margalit 1999). In terms of liberal thought, the 'discovery' of the economy as a separate realm is especially important because of the way in which it fuses into a single schema private or personal interest *and* the public or social good. As Smith put it, 'by acting according to the dictates of our moral faculties we necessarily pursue the most effectual means for promoting the happiness of mankind' (Smith 1982: 166). Until the 'discovery' of the invisible hand, liberal thinkers were far from convinced that the pursuit of private interests would lead to the advancement of the public or social good (Hundert 1977).

In terms of the pursuit of private economic interests, the economic realm is conceived as a realm of individual freedom. It provides a space for individuals to pursue and satisfy their private interests. This connects with liberal thought both in terms if its individualism and its commitment to forms of 'neutrality': individuals are the best judge of their own social welfare, and the market provides an institutional expression of the diversity of individual choices (Peacock and Rowley 1972). And it is because people are the best judges of their choices that the state should not intervene in the market to constrain those choices unnecessarily. The great historical 'trick' of liberal economic thought has been to combine this account of the economic realm with an account that stressed how the pursuit of private interests is congruent with, and can advance, the public good (Gauthier 1986). The first and most obvious way in which this is thought to happen is through the operation of the market mechanism. 'The superiority of market society over its predecessors and rivals is manifest in its capacity to ... direct mutual unconcern to mutual benefit' (Gauthier 1986: 102). The market provides the most efficient and socially beneficial allocation of scarce economic resources, and so everyone will benefit in the long run. Second, the dispositions the market cultivates in persons are sometimes thought to have broader social and political benefits. One of these is that the focus on commerce turns people away from other passions that might threaten a liberal order (Hirschman 1977, 1982). Another is that the market creates certain virtues – honesty, reliability, hard work – which are valuable for society in general (Hirschman 1982: 1465).

These two arguments, one about the significance of private freedom and the other about the 'public good', provide key liberal justifications for a liberal capitalist economy. There have, of course, been very extensive debates about what exactly public authorities should do to ensure that the market mechanism actually advances the public good while at the same time guaranteeing a realm of individual freedom. Even the most hardened advocates of the free market have accepted that some kinds of rules and some kinds of ordering institutions are necessary for the market to function effectively. It is here that most of the intellectual energy has been expended within the discipline of economics. There have been extensive debates over exactly which public goods the state should provide in order for the market to function effectively, and over the extent and type of regulation and intervention the state should undertake. This illustrates the long-standing liberal anxiety that left unfettered the operation of private interests in the economic sphere would in fact prevent the market from producing socially beneficial outcomes. The most obvious concern here has been with monopoly interests and concentrations of wealth and property (Peacock and Rowley 1972). This already suggests that it takes often quite extensive and detailed regulation of the economic realm to make the pursuit of private interests chime with the advancement of the public good.

Despite the obvious importance of the economic sphere in liberal thought, there is also a strand of liberal thinking that sees the economic spheres as a potential threat to liberal ends. There is first an anxiety that a focus on material welfare could lead to the erosion of individual freedom (Peacock and Rowley 1972: 480). This is the significance of various anti-poverty proposals such as income redistribution schemes or the extension of certain kind of democratic procedures to economic life (such as worker control), all of which hinge on the threat that the market may pose to the ability of persons to truly exercise their freedom (Nagel 1991: ch. 7; Crocker 1977). Within liberal thought there has also been recognition that certain aspects of social life should be insulated from the hard calculus of the market. For example, Dworkin has argued against the idea that the agencies of government, including the court system, should make decisions based solely on the basis of utilitarian principles of social welfare (Dworkin 1985b). Both Adam Smith and John Stuart Mill were concerned about the impact of market relations on personal virtues. Smith proposed certain government schemes to prevent the erosion of intellectual and martial virtues in the working population, while Mill feared the competitive individualism would erode the virtues of sympathy and altruism (Smith 1976: 781–4, 1978: 541; see also Audi 1998).

Underneath all of this theorizing about the economy, however, lies a deeper and more profound ambivalence. This is over whether the traits exhibited in the market are natural or not. That is, ultimately does the economic sphere rest on certain traits of human nature? Much of contemporary mainstream economics has tended to avoid this question. Instead, it has only assumed that individuals exhibit preferences that are stable and can be ranked. This is all that is needed, so the argument goes, to establish much of neoclassical economics (Blaug 1980). In addition, economists have tended to fall back on the argument that it does not really matter if the assumptions of economics are true, only that the theories that are derived from them 'work' (Friedman 1953). All this may be well and good for professional economists, but the question matters more in situations when effectively functioning markets do not yet exist. For the issue here becomes whether these traits simply have to be 'liberated' or whether they have to be constructed. To put it another way, does economics describe a universally possible or a sociologically particular way of organizing areas of social life?

All these tensions and ambiguities are reproduced in the World Bank's thinking about the economy and development. Structural adjustment hinged on the idea that economically rational behaviour was simply waiting to be released from the constraints imposed by an over-centralized state; yet at the same time the Bank has been engaging in extensive activities seemingly designed to 'educate' people in this behaviour. Despite this, the Bank is quite willing to endorse the basic liberal arguments for a market economy – that it is an important realm of individual freedom and mechanism for promoting the public good. But it only works as such a mechanism if the state plays a central role in constructing the institutions and practices that underpin it. Finally, the World Bank is concerned that large areas of the public sphere are insulated from the pursuit of private interests. In so doing the Bank replicates the attempt to demarcate a public and a private realm, and allocate the pursuit of public and private interests to these realms.

Civil society

The term 'civil society' has enjoyed a remarkable renaissance in recent years (Keane 1998; Seligman 1992; Cohen and Arato 1992). 'Civil society' holds an important place in liberal thought, signalling as it does an associational sphere somehow between the state and the family, which is both a realm of freedom (rights of association, worship and pursuit of varied goods) and a check on the power of the state. In the traditional liberal story civil society plays three important roles (Chambers and Kymlicka 2002). First, civil society advances liberal ends by providing a check on the centralizing or overbearing state. It does this by being an arena of free debate and criticism of the state. For civil society to be effective in this role, political resources such as wealth, leadership and organizational skills must be relatively widely dispersed through society. This is one connection between civil society and a liberal economy, as a liberal economy allows for at least some of these resources to be developed outside of control by the state. Second, civil society supports liberalism by providing an arena for diverse interests and opinions to develop. This, so the argument goes, prevents the formation of a tyrannical majority and allows for the expression in associational life of diverse life patterns. Third, civil society cultivates certain personal virtues and moral dispositions that are seen as important for sustaining liberal life. These include self-control, law-abidingness, cooperation, tolerance, and self-reliance. This role for civil society emphasizes the 'civil' aspects of civil society (Rosenblum 1989; Putnam 1995).

There are, of course, tensions and ambiguities that complicate this traditional picture. These cluster around three interrelated areas. First, there is a tension between civil society as a realm of private interests and as a protector of the public interest. As has been noted above, the traditional liberal story has it that civil society is both a realm of private interest and a realm where the public interest is advanced and protected. It is a realm of interests in the sense that groups form to advance economic and other interests in a relatively free context. These 'interest groups' (to use the contemporary political science language) engage in strategies, such as lobbying and publicity campaigns in order to advance their own particular interests. At the same time, however, civil society is charged with protecting the public interest through criticism of the government and free debate; and this would seem to require individuals to put aside their private interests and act instead in the interests of the larger polity. Again here we see the characteristic tension between the 'public' and the 'private'.

A second set of related ambiguities surrounds the role or status of 'identity' in civil society. The dilemma can easily be seen by thinking of 'affective' groups, such as those based on race, ethnicity, religion or culture. To the extent that these groups' internal values and arrangements are non-liberal (for example, they may be based on gender inequalities) should they be accepted as legitimate part of civil society? For some liberals the answer must be no (Kateb 1994; Galston 1995). Others have seen some value in these groups, although even here there tend to be limitations (Kymlicka 1991; B. Barry 2001). As Kymlicka has argued, 'liberals are committed to supporting the right of individuals *to decide for themselves* which aspects of their cultural heritage are worth passing on' (Kymlicka 1992: 144, emphasis added). The third set of ambiguities surrounds exactly what kinds of areas of public life are to be influenced or shaped by civil society (Charney 1998). That is, how much faith should liberals put in civil society to advance and protect liberalism, and how much should liberals seek guarantees outside of civil society – say in the state and the legal system – for liberal ends and arrangements? This is the flip side of the tension noted above over the extent to which the state should be insulated from society so as to be able to pursue liberal ends, and it follows from the anxieties over the extent to which the public interests can really be guaranteed by civil society.

The World Bank again exactly reproduces these tensions. It has found civil society in some of the most unlikely places and afforded it a significant role in the development of good governance; yet it must be the right kind of civil society (modern non-affective) and it must relate to the state in the right kind of way (public interest). These ambiguities point again to the idea of liberalism as a project of social transformation. Civil society is itself (at least partly) a constructed realm. Certain groups with certain kinds of identities and certain kinds of objectives are to be encouraged and other groups dismissed as 'bad civil society' (Chambers and Kopstein 2001). The pursuit of certain kinds of particularist interests (tribe, religion) are to be excluded, particularly from public policy making, yet the pursuit of other kinds of interests – economic for example – are to be encouraged as a way of making the state accountable.

Individualism and universalism

The individual lies at the heart of liberal theory. First, liberals have wanted to argue that liberal ends and arrangements are 'good' for the individuals who live within them. Liberalism is justified on the basis of what it will do for individuals. It is not that liberals have been unconcerned with 'society' or 'culture', but they have typically taken the ethical demands of these realms as being secondary to the claims of individuals (Kymlicka 1991). Second, liberal theorizing is individualist in the sense that it has typically proceeded 'bottom up' as it were; by delineating certain characteristics of individuals and then showing the desirability of certain institutional arrangements for those individuals. Third, the 'liberation' of the individual from the oppressions of 'tradition', culture and religion is at the heart of the traditional account of liberalism as a historical force.

Much of liberal theory rests on the idea that once the 'real' nature of persons has been identified, it will be possible to generate arguments about desirable political and social arrangements. Within liberal thought, 'individuals are pictured ... as given, with given interests, wants, purposes, needs, etc.; while society and the state are pictured as sets of actual or possible social arrangements which respond to those individuals' requirements' (Lukes 1973: 71). Not only are individuals conceived of (for theoretical purposes) as pre-existing the state and society, but the particular traits they have are understood to be invariant and universal. In turn this implies that the social arrangements desirable for this kind of person are also universally desirable. Almost all liberal thinkers have aspired to ground liberal theory in some kind of universal claim about the nature of persons. As Kant puts it, true morality 'already dwells in natural sound understanding and needs not so much to be taught as only to be clarified' (Kant 1997: 10). Liberal thinkers have differed on what about the nature of persons, exactly, provides the grounds for liberal social arrangements. But the most common account yokes together liberty or autonomy, with reason. The liberal account of the individual 'implies the centrality of the value of autonomy in the liberal scheme of things ... that a way of life which is determined by individuals is preferable to a way of life which is externally imposed' (Mendus 1989: 87–8). In turn this autonomy is 'frequently linked with the commitment to sustained rational examination of self, others and social practices' (Galston 1995: 521). Liberty or autonomy provides the necessary space for reason to work; and reason provides the answer to what to do with autonomy. This is why decisions about what to do are cast within liberal thought as choices; they are the result of a reasoned examination of alternatives. Straightaway it is clear how this links up with arguments for the neutral state, as the state must be neutral to ensure autonomy and respect the exercise of reason. It also links up with some of the justifications for a market economy and the importance of civil society, for these are the appropriate associational realms for this kind of individual.

Some contemporary liberal political philosophy has tried to ground itself in various non-universal commitments. This is evident, for example, in the debate over whether John Rawls' *Theory of Justice* rests on 'metaphysical' or 'political' commitments (Rawls 1985). It is also evident in the so-called 'post-modern' liberalism of Richard Rorty (Rorty 1983, 1993). A first response to this is to say that the difficulty liberal thought has with avowedly non-universal commitments can be seen in the anxieties these suggestions provoke among other liberal thinkers. Brian Barry, Thomas Pogge and Richard Dworkin among others have wanted to reassert the universalism of (at least some) liberal commitments (B. Barry 2001; Pogge 2000; Dworkin 1996). A second response is to say that even this supposedly non-universal liberalism is ambiguous about the extent to which it is really prepared to abandon at least some kind of universalism. This is evidenced for example by Rawls' claim that 'a concern for human rights should be a fixed part of the foreign policy of liberal societies' (Rawls 1993b: 80). The final point to note about this is that, certainly historically, liberalism was not afflicted by these kinds of anxieties. And, as we shall see, in terms of the World Bank's political practices, these positions seem a long way off. It seems safe to say that, in general at least, liberalism's claims are grounded in an account of individuals, and that the claims about the characteristics of individuals that provide liberalism with its foundations are universalist in theoretical ambition.

One of the things that follows from this general theoretical orientation is what we might call a 'geographical universalism'.[2] Given that all people, everywhere, are the same (they have the same 'nature'), all people everywhere would benefit from liberal social arrangements. There is no place on the planet that liberals think is somehow 'off-limits', at least in principle. Of course, the extent to which liberals have been able to pursue liberal ends in different parts of the world has been conditioned by a host of factors. But that should not cast into doubt liberalism's genuinely universal vision. If liberalism is cosmopolitan, it is also profoundly and abidingly judgemental – how could it not be, given that liberals believe themselves to be in possession of the truth about social and political affairs? People, societies, and cultures are to be judged by the extent to which they live up to the standards of conduct arrived at in liberal theory (Hindess 2002b). And it is this that ultimately drives the liberal project; for being in possession of a truth for all means liberals cannot rest easy simply in the knowledge that they are right; they must attempt, if they can, to foist this on everyone else. It is in this sense that Beate Jahn is right to say that liberal thought has always been imperialist (Jahn 2005). The point is not that all colonialism was liberal; it is that (almost) all liberalism is colonial in aspiration. The distinctions liberal thinkers have made between the 'civilized and uncivilized', for example, illustrate exactly this kind of geographical universalism (Jahn 2005; Gong 1984). The varied 'rankings' of countries produced today in terms how 'free' they are, or what their 'human rights' record is, continue this tradition; as, of course, does the idea of 'developed' and 'less-developing' countries. And this in turn inspires and legitimates attempts to make people and places more 'free', more developed or more 'civilized'.

This is not the place to discuss whether the kind of theoretical universalism – the 'view from nowhere' – to which liberalism aspires is really possible (Nagel 1986). The answer to this obviously has an important bearing on the normative question we raised at the end of the Introduction. Suffice it to say that many liberal thinkers clearly think it is, and much liberal practice is based on the idea that, somehow, the desire to change the way people in other places think about themselves and their social relations is justified.

Despite (or perhaps because of) the centrality of the individual in liberal theory, liberal thought has in fact been decidedly ambivalent about people. While liberalism has tried to ground its project in the 'true' nature of persons, as a matter of sociology, liberals have doubted whether these persons really existed. The stress on autonomy and reason that lies at the heart of much liberal thought is countered by the continual stress on how malleable people actually are; how influenced they are by custom, tradition, and religion. Despite liberalism seeming to celebrate the individual, much of liberal thought has taken a very dim view of what people are actually like. Given the liberals' belief in the correctness of their prescriptions, it may be inevitable that the actual messy lived lives of real people will continually disappoint them. But as we have been at pains to point out, liberals are not content to be disappointed, they really want to change these lives. And this is where liberalisms' individualism is double-edged. For the achievement of liberalism requires enmeshing people in a complex set of disciplines.

The liberal project

As we have argued, liberals want to change the world. What makes liberalism a project of social transformation is that there is within it a consistent concern with *how* to change the world. One part of this is what will be called here the 'sociological' aspects of liberal thought. This is the concern with identifying the actual practices and beliefs of people and groups, and of identifying where those practices and beliefs stand in the way of the achievement of liberal ends. This generates perhaps the most fundamental tension within liberal thought: that between nature and culture. For in identifying the reasons why people thought and acted as they did, liberal thinkers called into question the extent to which people exhibited the 'natural' traits (reason, autonomy) that were supposed to ground liberalism.

The examples of John Locke, Adam Smith and John Stuart Mill help to illustrate the point. John Locke had a persistent concern with what he saw as a widespread and general failure to see that the kinds of arguments he advocated were correct. He argued that even when arguments were plainly laid before people who did have the ability and time to reason correctly, they often lacked the right criteria of judgement. This was because they were under the influence of a 'prevailing passion', or they yielded assent to the 'common received opinions of either [their] friends, or party; neighbourhood or country' (Tully 1988a: 31).[3] As Locke asked in his 'Letter to Tom', 'When did ever any truth settle itself in anyone's mind by the strength and authority of its own evidence?' Rather, 'men live upon trust, and their knowledge is nothing but opinion moulded up between custom and interest' (Locke 1993a: 140). 'Mankind is supported in the ways of virtue or vice by the society he is of, and the conversation he keeps, example and fashion being the great governors of this world' (Locke 1993c: 232).[4] It seems Locke thought that 'assent [was] governed by non-rational factors; by passion, custom, and education' (Tully 1988a: 31).

The significance and power of these factors in English political life was evident to Locke because men had accepted the principle of the Divine Right of Kings. This was not only false, but had 'exposed all subjects to the utmost misery of tyranny and oppression' (Locke 1989: 4). Because men desired to avoid the 'pains and trouble of thinking and examining for themselves', Locke wrote, 'they mix with their religious worship and speculative opinions other doctrines absolutely destructive to the society wherein they live' (Locke 1996: 169, 1993d: 197). Locke was acutely aware that people were persuaded by works which were wrong, dangerous or incomprehensible. Explaining his decision to publish *An Essay on Human Understanding*, Locke says that knowledge would have been 'very much more advanced in the world, if the endeavours of ingenious and industrious men had not been much cumbered with the learned but frivolous use of uncouth, affected or unintelligible terms' (Locke 1976: xliii). This theme is also present in his criticisms of Filmer. There was 'noise' and 'applause' following the publication of *Patriarcha*, despite the fact, that, according to Locke, Filmer 'cross[es] the rule of language' and his 'way of writing [involves] huddling several suppositions together, and that in doubtful and general terms makes such a medley and confusion, that it is impossible to show his mistakes' (Locke 1989: 3, 15). Locke's sociology depicted the mass of men as ignorant or under the influence of custom, fashion and tradition. The political dangers this posed were clear as it led to the acceptance of false and dangerous doctrines which threatened the constancy and moderation of desires which, John Dunn has argued, Locke thought necessary if the political institutions he advocated were to function successfully (Dunn 1984).

We find a related argument in the work of Adam Smith. On the one hand Smith says that the 'desire of bettering our condition ... comes with us from the womb, and never leaves us till we go to the grave' (Smith 1976: 314). It is, he famously said, 'not from the benevolence of the butcher, the brewer or the baker that we expect our dinner, but from their regard for their own interest' (Smith 1976: 26–7). This would seem to suggest that the traits exhibited by economic man were natural. Smith did not reduce all of human action to the search for material gain. He accepted that all sorts of 'passions' could move men to action, including desire for recognition, praise and good standing with our peers (Smith 1982). He did, however, seem to suggest that economic man was in some sense natural, and thus that the primary objective of the government should be to 'liberate' this man from undue restrictions on his desire to 'truck, barter and exchange one thing for another' (Smith 1976).

In his more 'sociological' moments, however, Smith argued that these natural traits would only in fact be exhibited by men under quite restricted conditions. For example, Smith identified the existence of large landholdings as significant barriers to the operation of these traits.[5] It 'seldom happens', Smith argued, 'that a great proprietor is a great improver':

> to improve land, like all other commercial projects, requires an exact attention to small savings and small gains, of which a man born to a great fortune is seldom capable. The situation of such a person naturally disposes him to attend rather to ornament which pleases his fancy than to profit for which he has so little occasion.
>
> (Smith 1976: 385)

Smith's attack on these large estates was based on the twin notions of ownership and improvement (Vogel: 1988). While these estates were 'owned', the laws of inheritance prevented them from being broken into smaller land holdings and sold. Large land holdings were a barrier to improvement because the land owner could have no real need or desire for more money. 'One great hindrance to the progress of agriculture is the throwing of great tracts of land into the hands of single persons' (Smith 1978: 522). It is only when the plots are broken up and sold to smaller cultivators that there is any incentive to improve the land (Smith 1978: 469). These examples indicate that what Smith really thought desirable were arrangements which placed 'the individual under the right kind of psychic tension'. He thought individuals would apply themselves to improvement, and hence advance the general happiness of mankind, when the 'reward for effort [was] neither too low (slaves) nor too great (monopolists, large land-owners)' (Rosenberg 1960: 559). This casts serious doubt on the economy as a natural order, for it seems that Smith thought that the necessary attitudes will emerge only under quite specific institutional arrangements which Smith did not think were completely in place.

In attempting to explain how John Stuart Mill, the great champion of freedom and equality, could have ended up justifying British colonialism, Bhikhu Parekh has argued that within his work there was a 'profound tension' between 'what human beings tended to do and what they ought to do' (Parekh 1995: 93). That is, there was tension between Mill's 'sociolog-ical' or 'anthropological' observations about actual persons and their actions, both in Britain and India, and his theoretical arguments about the way persons should think and act. Mill described the colonial government of India as 'a government of foreigners, over a people most difficult to understand, and still more difficult to be improved' (Mill 1990: 155). Part of the difficulty in 'improving' India stemmed from the fact that the 'hindoo [sic] state of mind ... reproduc[ed] in so many respects the mental characteristics of the infancy of the human race' (quoted in Zastoupil 1994: 174). According to Martin Moir, Mill saw the Indian people as 'too passive, and too crushed by centuries of despotism, to take an active stand in defence of their individual legal and political rights' and they 'were too dominated by custom as the "final appeal"' (Moir 1990: xlii). Similar themes are again present in Mill's domestic writings. Here Mill also stressed the power of custom and fashion. He said that the 'rules which obtain among' the 'major-ity', 'appear to themselves to be self-evident and self-justifying', but this 'universal illusion is one of the examples of the magical influence of custom' (Mill 1976: 64). In discussing the dangers inherent in representative govern-ment, Mill identified 'general ignorance and incapacity, or, to speak more moderately, insufficient mental qualifications in the controlling body', and the 'danger of its being under the influence of interests not identical with the general welfare of the community' (Mill 1972: 262).

The examples of Locke, Smith and John Stuart Mill point to a general tension within liberal thought between 'nature' and 'culture'. We should understand the identification of those features of social life (tradition, reli-gion, elites) that hinder the establishment of liberal ends and arrangements as a key feature of liberalism's political project. This identification, and the mismatch between what people actually think and do, and what liberals think they should think and do, helps to explain a characteristic feature of liberal thought: the tendency to appeal to almost entirely abstract arguments to justify liberal ends and arrangements. In some instances, where people's actions or preferences seemed to support what these thinkers deemed to be desirable arrangements, they *were* appealed to provide support for these justifications. For example, Locke was prepared to use evidence of the wide variety of customs and beliefs to support his claim that persons had no innate capacity to distinguish right from wrong (Grant 1988; Batz 1974). What should be clear, however, is that this appeal to the actual actions and thoughts of people cannot do the theoretical 'work' in the arguments for desirable ends and arrangements. Any appeal to empirical 'facts' has to be limited to illustrative purposes, because the vast body of these thinkers sociological observations showed that people were generally in ignorance of what was good for them. Liberal thinkers have then typically employed theoretical devices to 'strip away' this body of sociological observations in their arguments for desirable ends and arrangements. Appeal is made instead to the actions and preferences of some non-actual person in some highly circumscribed circumstances. The most obvious of these is the 'state of nature' in its various guises, including in modern liberal theory (the 'original position', 'veil of ignorance').

Liberalism's search for firm foundations in nature or reason, or whatever, has taken it far away from what it has identified as the actual habits, actions and practices of persons. It is precisely this distance that provides the key to understanding liberalism as a project of social transformation. For arguments grounded on universal human nature provide the justification for closing the gap, and liberalism's sociology provides the resources for thinking about how this is to be done.

Again Locke, Smith and John Stuart Mill are illustrative. James Tully has demonstrated how Locke systematically constructed a set of ideas and recommended practices which would govern not only men's beliefs, but also their actions in detailed ways (Tully 1988a). Locke made a distinction between the mass of mankind who would remain in a more or less permanent state of ignorance, and those who did have the time and ability to reason correctly but often failed to do so. The basis of Locke's disciplinary project for the poor was the inculcation habits of thought and action through the calibrated use of rewards and punishment (Tully 1988a: 39–42). This can be seen in his report to the Board of Trade on reform of the poor law system (Locke 1993e). Locke argued that the 'growth of the poor' was caused by nothing else but the relaxation of discipline and corruption of manners. To overcome this, the various categories of people receiving parish relief were to be exposed to varying degrees of 'discipline', including hard labour, whipping, being enlisted in the navy, transportation and spending time in houses of correction or 'working-schools'. This was a way of making the poor 'useful to the public'. The children of the poor were 'to be inured to work, which is of no small consequence to the making of them sober and industrious all their lives after' (Locke 1993e: 446, 543). The aim of Locke's recommendations, according to Tully, was to,

> deconstruct old customary ways of life and to produce new ones ... to use the law, the navy, corporal punishment, the threats of divine punishment, economic incentives, and the activity of repetitious labour, from the age of three onwards, to fabricate an individual who is habituated to docility and useful labour.
>
> (Tully 1988a: 68)

Locke did not think that 'right assent' would flow directly from a rational demonstration of true principles, even for that portion of the population who did have the time and ability to reason correctly. Thus he argued that it would be necessary to develop in these persons an artificial inclination or passion to suspend, examine, and assent in accordance with the correct grounds. This required a 'fundamental and massive educational project in which reason ... must be "bound" and molded' (Mehta 1992: 125) Underlying this project were educational practices that would form these mental inclinations. The most important of these is the notion of habituation which was also central to Locke's disciplinary project for the poor. The significance of habituation is explained by the recognition that force or coercion is ineffective in changing the way men think. 'Compulsion ... cannot alter men's minds', 'punishment and fear may make men dissemble, but, not convincing anybody's reason, cannot possibly make them assent to the opinion' (Locke 1993d: 192, 206). It is necessary then to form and govern men's actions through the inculcation of habits. 'Practice must settle the habit of doing without reflecting on the rule', and 'children are not to be taught by rules, which will be always slipping out of their memories. What you think necessary for them to do, settle in them by an indispensable practice ... this will beget habits in them, which, once being established, operate of themselves easily and naturally without the assistance of memory' (Locke 1996: 175, 40). Another educational practice was to govern men's thoughts by appealing to reputation and fashion (Mehta 1992: 148–54). 'He ... that would govern the world well, had need consider what fashions he makes than what laws; and to bring anything into use he need only give it reputation' (Locke 1993b: 237). 'Though force cannot master the opinions men have, not plant new ones in their breasts, yet courtesy, friendship, and soft usage may' (Locke 1993d: 206). As Joseph Carrig has argued, Locke's writings illustrate an 'attempt to create a new kind of individual' (Carrig 2001). Locke was concerned to show how people who were governed by opinion, custom, habit and fashion could be made more fitted to the kind of liberal society he advocated. They could be made this way by harnessing precisely those things which had kept them in ignorance of desirable political and social arrangements in the first place.

As we noted above, Adam Smith seemed to argue that while there may be certain universal traits of human nature, these are only apparent under quite specific circumstances. Importantly, Smith makes the acquisition of the 'most essential parts of education', reading, writing, accounting (basic numeracy) one of the duties of the sovereign, because there is 'scarce a trade which does not afford some opportunities' of applying them. Smith goes so far as to suggest that the public (sovereign) can impose upon

> almost the entire body of the people the necessity of acquiring those most essential parts of education, by obliging every man to undergo an examination or probation in them before he can obtain the freedom in any corporation, or be allowed to set up any trade either in a village or town.
>
> (Smith 1976: 786)

Smith also thought the education of elites was important. For them he advocated the 'study of science and philosophy' and argued that the state should render this 'almost universal among all people of middling or more than middling rank and fortune'. 'Science is the great antidote to the poison of enthusiasm and superstition; and where all the superior ranks of people were secured from it, the inferior ranks could not be much exposed to it' (Smith 1976: 796). In fact Smith advocated a 'radical programme of enactment and demolition' at both the legislative and institutional levels (Winch 1983). In this light, his arguments about the invisible hand and the natural desire of people to pursue their interests are best seen as rhetorical and persuasive (Bazerman 1993). They establish not how the world is, but how it should be. The rest of his arguments are about why the world as it is does not conform to these ideals and what should be done about this

For John Stuart Mill, 'improvement had to be cultivated, not merely imposed, and this required heeding the thoughts, perceptions, feelings and prejudices of those the British wished to change'. Mill sought to fashion this knowledge into useful information for controlling and influencing the thoughts and actions of Indians (Zastoupil 1994: 174, 192). In particular, the recognition that Indian society was hierarchical could be used to assist in the eradication of 'barbarous practices'. In discussing infanticide, Mill commends the engagement of 'influential persons of caste to preserve their own children, and to aid in enforcing the same conduct on others' (Mill 1990: 122). Mill certainly thought that traditional caste authority was part of the reason for the persistence of these prejudices, nonetheless, he thought it could also be enlisted in their eradication. Speaking more generally, Mill says that 'the triumph which has been effected over the religious prejudices of the natives ... is a proof that this indirect mode of correcting their superstitions ... is a highly effective one' (Mill 1990: 147). That is, for Mill the correction of India's prejudices was not to be accomplished by either coercion or through rational persuasion, but rather by harnessing some of those social patterns which had kept the Indian people in ignorance in the first place.

Locke, Smith and John Stuart Mill were all concerned to provide some account of how actual persons could be brought to see what was right, or at least to act in accordance with what was right. For these thinkers it was the identification of those things which had kept people in ignorance in the first place that provided the resources for this transformation. Public opinion, education, habit, and gullibility could all be harnessed to this project. Viewed in this light, to the extent that liberalism is 'individualistic', this is distinctly double edged. On the one hand liberalism holds out the possibility that both persons and their contexts could be 'improved'; and this is the emancipatory promise of liberalism. On the other hand, as the barriers to progressive transformation were largely to be found in the characteristics and behaviour of actual persons, so these persons would bear the brunt of any transformative project. To be sure liberalism is about liberating people from certain 'oppressive' institutions and practices but it does so only by creating new forms of discipline.

Liberal spheres and the liberal project

We can now return to the liberal spheres we discussed earlier in the chapter. We noted in each case a set of tensions and ambiguities, and we can now relate these more systematically to the idea of liberalism as a project of social transformation. The central ambiguity about the state in liberal thought – that it must be both weak and strong – makes sense when liberal thought about the state is seen as part of a more extended reflection of the possibility and desirability of social transformation. For the state is cast as the most significant instrument of social transformation. As we can see with Locke, Smith and Mill above, the state is charged with a whole range of tasks all of which require it to be strong, relatively autonomous and capable of intricate interventions into social life. Of course this kind of state is a potential threat to the liberal order too, and so the state must be controlled and constrained from pursuing interventions that run counter to the achievement of liberalism. What this suggests is that the 'liberal state' will be characterized by a series of institutional mechanism designed to create this delicate balance between intervention on behalf of liberalism and non-intervention in liberalism.

The liberal project also implies the engineering of the economy and civil society. These associational realms are in that sense not independent from the state, rather they are at least in part the product of the actions of the state in its attempt to create liberalism. In addition these realms must be regulated carefully by the state to ensure that they do indeed produce the kinds of benefits liberal theory expects of them.

Conclusion

This chapter has been concerned to sketch out the idea that liberalism can be understood as a project of social transformation. This is at odds with conventional understanding of liberalism as a body of normative political philosophy. Of course, such philosophizing is an important aspect of liberalism, but this chapter has argued that there are other elements of liberal thought that point to it being a political project. First, liberalism's universalism legitimates and justifies attempts to create liberal ends. Second, we identified within liberal thought a persistent concern with identifying what stands in the way of the achievement of liberalism, and a persistent concern with various techniques that might overcome these barriers. That is liberal thinkers were thinking about social transformation. The chapter also identified how an understanding of liberalism as a political project helps make sense of various characteristic features of liberal thought, such as the use of theoretical devices like the state of nature, and perennial ambiguities about what counts as 'civil society'.

The chapter has remained at the level of theory; much of the rest of the book is about examining what this kind of project of social transformation looks like when expressed through the political agency of the World Bank. The chapter has also remained focused on domestic transformation. This is important because what the World Bank is engaged in is a project of domestic transformation in developing countries. But to understand how an international organization like the World Bank has come to be able to pursue this kind of project, we need to consider how it became institutionalized in international politics.

2 The World Bank, sovereignty and development

This chapter examines the foundation and early history of the World Bank. It is not, however, a straightforward institutional history of the Bank. Certainly some of the institutional characteristics of the World Bank are central to explaining the kinds of relations it has had with its borrower countries over the years. These features, however, reflected much broader institutional and normative shifts within international society.

First, there had been long-running series of shifts in the way sovereignty was understood. The achievement of state sovereignty in the post-war world was distinctly double-edged. Sovereignty represented the institutionalization of a notion of collective freedom (captured under the name 'self-determination') but it also represented a set of expectations about what countries were to do with their new-found freedom; and, in turn, a set of expectations about what the governments of these countries were to do for their people. To use Reus-Smit's phrase, development had become one of the 'moral purposes' of the state (Reus-Smit 1999). This in turn helped to generate a particular view of the role of the state in the development process. The sovereign state was the vehicle for the achievement of development, but the state (government) was to be the primary agent of development. Second, the World Bank represented the *international institutionalization* of this broad normative shift. For the first time public international organisations were established to assist countries in the pursuit of development. This is part of an ambitious attempt to institutionalize a liberal international order after the end of the Second World War. In this order, the moral obligation to pursue development became overlain by a series of essentially prudential arguments about the links between economic development and political stability.

The third shift was the rise of development economics. The years after 1945 witnessed the emergence and professionalization of 'development expertise', derived in large part from the trajectory of economics as a specialized discipline with a claim to a particular kind of neutral knowledge. The problem of development was understood as largely an economic problem, to be understood and resolved through the application of analytical tools derived from economic theory. The claim to possess special expertise has remained a constant feature of the World Bank's self-image and the kind of cognitive arrogance this claim embodies continues to shape the way the Bank relates to its borrower countries. In the early years of the Bank's operations, however, the Bank generally only concerned itself with specific project lending. This was driven by an account of how lending for specific projects (infrastructure, power generation and so on) would lead to economic development, but it was also shaped by the fact that the World Bank was established as a kind of bank, and at least in the years up to the 1970s, this was important in conditioning the kind of lending the Bank undertook.

Taken together these shifts shaped the way the Bank related to its borrower countries. But they also created a series of tensions that are important for the emergence of a more interventionist development policy in the 1980s and 1990s. First, of course, there was a tension between sovereignty as freedom and sovereignty as obligation, especially given that international institutions like the World Bank were committed to assisting countries fulfil their developmental obligations. This established the possibility that when states were seen as having failed in this obligation, sovereignty is trumped by the pursuit of development by international agencies like the World Bank. Second, and related, while the World Bank and indeed almost all other development agencies concerned themselves with only a narrow range of issues, their development thinking was powered by the idea that they really did know what was best for these countries. There is the possibility here that, should development agencies start to concern themselves with a much wider range of issues, they would feel justified in pursuing much more interventionist development policies. And both of these things started to happen in the late 1970s.

Sovereignty and self-determination

Post-colonial states were born into an international institutional context that placed all kinds of demands on them. Most importantly, as Reus-Smit has argued, 'legitimate statehood and rightful state action were ... increasingly tied to the augmentation of individuals' purposes and potentialities' (Reus-Smit 1999: 121). That is, into the normative structure of international politics had emerged the view that it was, in the end, individual persons and their well-being that provided the only legitimate foundation for state sovereignty. Sovereignty, in this order was only ambiguously a realm of freedom. It was certainly a realm of freedom in some respects – although it is clear that the kind of sovereignty many of the newly-independent states were granted was historically unusual (Jackson 1993). But it was also a concept laden with expectations about the kinds of things states should do with their new-found freedom, and, in turn, a set of expectations about the kinds of things the governments of these states should be doing for and on behalf of their societies.

The concept of sovereignty has become a matter of renewed interest within international relations (Biersteker and Weber 1996). The debate has tended to circle around two sets of concerns. First, realist and liberal interdependence theorists have examined the extent to which economic interdependence, technological change and the proliferation of non-state actors have eroded state sovereignty (Keohane and Nye 1972; Gilpin 1987; Zacher 1991). Second, 'critical' and 'constructivist' theorists, have historicized the concept of sovereignty, analyzed its place as an organizing and constitutive principle of the modern state system, and detailed the norms, rules and practices that go into sustaining it (Walker 1993; Der Derian 1987; Biersteker and Weber 1996). It has been an explicit aim of this kind of analysis to resist the idea that sovereignty can be defined outside of particular historical contexts. As Walker has argued, 'the very attempt to treat sovereignty as a matter of definition and legal principles encourages a certain amount of amnesia about its historical and culturally specific character' (Walker 1993: 166; see also Bartleson 1995: 13). Sovereignty *is* a matter of legal principles, of course, but in international political practice it is also a norm which has evolved and become bound up with other norms and commitments.

One of the most significant changes in the way sovereignty has been understood has been its increasing association with the idea of self-determination. This has had very important implications for how the legitimacy and role of the government in a sovereign state was understood. In the settlement of Westphalia the rights associated with territorial possession were claimed by and on behalf of sovereigns. The various treaties associated with the settlement did attempt to place some limits on what rulers could do within their territories (mostly concerned with allowing some degree of freedom of religious worship), but state sovereignty as it emerged alongside the consolidation of the European state system was largely about providing a principle that could regulate conduct between sovereigns (Ruggie 1986; Osiander 1994: ch. 2). This situation was transformed into one in which sovereignty is claimed by and on behalf of a people or nation, rather than a sovereign (Barkin and Cronin 1994). This is bound up with the dramatic change in the language of political argument in Europe, whereby appeals to the 'people', the 'public', 'public opinion' and 'civil society' become increasingly persuasive. The developments here are complex and multifaceted.

First there were a series of intellectual developments that stemmed in part from the kinds of liberal arguments about the role of the state and the existence of a society and an economy that we reviewed in the last chapter

(Taylor 1995). These played an important role in establishing the idea that a 'society' with its own internal dynamics exists before the establishment of a sovereign authority, and that, as Locke argued, in some (very few) cases the people had the right to act to preserve themselves in the face of tyrannical threats to their estates, liberties and lives. The emergence of the discourse of political economy, alongside the growth of capitalist economic relations, reinforced the idea that society was characterized by its own internal laws which give it an extra-political identity, and more importantly, contributed to the idea that the duty of the state was to provide the conditions for the advancement of the material well-being of its society (Taylor 1995: 215–6). This is a crucial element in the shift on the grounds of legitimacy for states. Second, as Habermas has shown, these intellectual developments were followed in the eighteenth century with social changes in Europe that produced a 'public' and 'public opinion' which both claimed, and was increasingly understood to have, an important role in monitoring and criticizing government activity and providing a space for the expression of political liberty (Habermas 1989; see also Volpa 1992). Third, and standing in a complex relationship to these developments was the emergence of ideas of nationalism and national identity. What all of these shifts pointed to was the idea (although of course not the reality) that 'society' or the 'nation' existed prior to, or at least was ontologically more basic than, the state.

This changed understanding of the relationship between the state and its 'society' ('people', 'nation') contributed to a transformation in the political imagination of Western Europe. The emergence into international politics of these ideas came through the idea of national self-determination. There emerged a close connection between the idea of state sovereignty and the claim for self-determination where being self-determining as a people largely came to mean possession of sovereign statehood (Higgins 1994: ch. 7). This raised the difficult question of what constituted a people who were entitled to self-determination, but part of the close connection between self-determination and sovereignty was the more or less fictitious view that those within sovereign states were or would become a 'people', and that this identity formed the basis of a claim for sovereign statehood. As the UN Declaration on the Granting of Independence to Colonial Countries and Peoples puts it, 'all peoples have a right to "self-determination"', and no 'inadequacy of political, economic, social, or educational preparedness should ... serve as a pretext for delaying [their] independence'. The other side of this claim was the idea that the state and government should in some important respects represent the wishes and aspirations of its people. The government or rulers became seen as the agency that could fulfil the promises of self-determination. Governments were to be seen as the 'expression' (in some sense) of the people. This is part of the reason why, in some instances, governments could be seen as illegitimate because they did not represent the wishes and aspirations of their society, and this is most obvious in arguments for decolonization (Higgins 1994: ch. 7). As James Mayall has argued, the nationalization of the concept of self-determination placed a time bomb under the concept of empire as a legitimate political form (Mayall 1989).

Once the idea emerged that the basis of sovereignty was a (more or less fictitious) claim to self-determination by or on behalf of a 'people', intervention in the affairs of other states took on a new significance because it would be intervention in the 'national project' of a nation, not simply a refusal to respect the territorial rights of rulers. Thus the normative claim of state sovereignty came to include the view that it was wrong in some moral or ethical, and not just legal, sense to intervene in a country's internal affairs. This reworking of the idea of sovereignty reproduces at the international level arguments about tolerance, pluralism and autonomy which have become increasingly characteristic of liberal political theory (see Beitz 1979). In international politics, however, these claims existed within an international institutional and normative structure that increasingly designated what were desirable domestic political and social arrangements. That is, while sovereignty and non-intervention remained very important norms in international politics, there was a significant strand of international thought and practice committed to the idea that the achievement of certain political ends within states might warrant the undermining or withholding of sovereignty.

This can be seen, for example, in the French and American Revolutions (Reus-Smit 1999: 127–9). These revolutions indicated that the nation state could now be a place for the achievement of the political ideals of Enlightenment liberalism (Mayall 1989). This gave the possession of sovereign statehood a new significance, but also potentially threatened the traditional substance of state sovereignty as Edmund Burke realized:

> The Treaty of Westphalia is, with France, an antiquated fable. The rights and liberty she was bound to maintain are now a system of wrong and tyranny which she is bound to destroy. Her good and ill dispositions are shown by the same means. To communicate peaceably the rights of men is the true mode of her showing her friendship; to force sovereigns to submit to those rights is her mode of showing hostility.
>
> (Quoted in Der Derian 1987: 171–2)

If the nation state was now a place for the achievement of liberal political and social arrangements, and these arrangements were universally desirable, there was an important justification, as Burke feared, for imposing them on other states. The diplomatic agents of the new French regime (at least in its early years) were 'to be not only gatherers of information, but disseminators of the Rights of Man' (Der Derian 1987: 176). The sense that possession of sovereign statehood was bound up with achieving good political and social arrangements also found expression in the 'standard of civilization' (Jackson 1993: 71–4; Gong 1984). During the nineteenth century a 'civilized' state permitted freedom of trade, applied the law in an egalitarian manner, accepted European international law, maintained diplomatic relations with other states, practised some degree of administrative efficiency, and generally upheld 'civilized' values. The standard of civilization provided colonizers with a paternal justification to rule over 'uncivilized' peoples and attempt, if possible, to 'civilize' them, at least until they were in a position to realize the promises of Enlightenment 'civilization' themselves. As John Stuart Mill put it, some nations had 'not got beyond the period during which it is likely to be for their benefit that they should be conquered and held in subjection by [civilized] foreigners' (Mill 1973: 337). The achievement of Enlightenment ideals within the nation state continued to underpin, among other things, the succession of international agreements on the abolition of the slave trade, and continues to underpin the contemporary discourse on human rights, the promotion of democracy, and humanitarian intervention (Barkin 1998; Donnelly 1999).

Running alongside this story about the relationship between liberalism and sovereignty has been a less familiar but very similar story about economic development. Being a sovereign state has become intimately bound up with the pursuit of a 'national economic project', and being the government of a sovereign state entails a duty to provide for the material well-being of the populace as a central component of 'the augmentation of individuals' purposes and potentialities'. This has become increasingly significant in the twentieth century with the massive expansion of government activities, the vast bulk of which are concerned with economic development and material well-being (Poggi 1990: ch. 7). As Thomas and Lauderdale have argued, within international society 'the state is chartered with the responsibility for "national welfare" ... which means a national economic policy that stimulates gross national product and a national welfare programme' (Thomas and Lauderdale 1988: 388).

By the time the World Bank was founded the possession of sovereignty was distinctly double-edged. On the one hand it promised a realm of freedom; freedom for the nation or society to pursue its ends without external control or intervention. On the other hand it came with its own obligations: as the freedom granted to sovereign states was in some sense grounded in a claim about a society or nation, so it also implied that the state (government) should act on behalf of, and in some sense for, that society or nation; and that a key part of this was the pursuit of 'development'.

Development and the liberal order

The World Bank was founded in 1944 as the International Bank for Reconstruction and Development. The purposes of this new organization, as laid out in its Articles of Agreement, were to 'assist in the reconstruction and development of territories of members by facilitating the investment of capital for productive purposes, ... the reconversion of productive facilities to peacetime needs and the encouragement of the development of productive facilities and resources in less developed countries'. The World Bank's contribution to post-war reconstruction in Europe was very limited. It made only four loans to European states for this purpose.[1] Compared to the scale of the problem, the new organization was woefully undercapitalized, and it was in any case superseded in this role by the Marshall Plan (Mikesell 1972). As Keynes had foreseen, however, the World Bank quickly became an organization devoted to the task of economic development in less developed countries:

> It is likely, in my judgment, that the field of reconstruction from the consequences of war will mainly occupy the proposed bank in its early days. But as soon as possible, and with increasing emphasis as time goes on, there is a second primary duty laid upon it, namely to develop the resources and productive capacities of the world, with special reference to the less developed countries.
>
> (Quoted in Mason and Asher 1972: 1–2)

This was a remarkable innovation in international politics (Fieldhouse 1999: part III; Arndt 1987: 22–9; Cooper 1997). It represented the idea that a public international organization should assist states in their national economic project.

The World Bank was only one of a number of institutions established under US hegemony after the Second World War. A number of commentators have argued this international order was a 'liberal order'. It has been called variously, 'structural liberalism', 'embedded liberalism', and the 'liberal moment' (Deudney and Ikenberry 1999; Ruggie 1982; Latham 1997). These views accept that an importantly different set of international institutions and practices was established under US hegemony and that these changed the character of inter-state relations, at least among those states within the liberal order. There is something importantly right about these arguments. Nonetheless, they share a common failure to take seriously the place of developing countries within the liberal order.

Daniel Deudney and G. John Ikenberry identify five features of the post-war order which together lead them to propose a theory of 'structural liberalism' that, they argue, characterizes 'an unusual and distinctive subsystem in world politics' (Deudney and Ikenberry 1999: 195). First they identify the prevalence of 'security co-binding' as opposed to the operation of the balance of power. Security co-binding is an attempt to tie states into institutions which mutually constrain their actions, and thereby reduce the effects of anarchy. The most notable of these institutions is NATO. Second, they suggest that while America was the most powerful state in the post-war order, its relations with other states were generally characterized by reciprocity and cooperation, a situation they describe as 'penetrated hegemony'. They argue that this has led to American hegemony being seen as highly legitimate. Third, they identify the existence of 'semi-sovereign and partial great powers', notably Germany and Japan. Both states have accepted the constraints imposed on their actions by the allies at the end of the Second World War. Fourth, they suggest that a key feature of the liberal order has been its economic openness which, so they argue, provides a high prospect of absolute gains and thus an incentive to mitigate anarchy. Finally, they argue that the particular 'civic identity' of Western states reinforces a common sense of identity and shared interests and practices among liberal states. Deudney and Ikenberry suggest that it is 'the overall pattern of these elements and their interaction that constitute the structure of the liberal order' (Deudney and Ikenberry 1999: 195).

John Ruggie has characterized the economic elements of the post-war order in terms of 'embedded liberalism' (Ruggie 1986). In line with his general theoretical position, Ruggie stresses the role which 'intersubjective understandings' played in the formation of the post-war order (Ruggie 1998). For Ruggie, the content of the post-war economic order is the result of a shared commitment on the part of the allies to a particular way of organizing relations between the domestic and international realms. This is what he calls embedded liberalism and it results from three kinds of intersubjective understandings. First, there was a change in what the role of public authorities in domestic politics was thought to be. There was a recognition that the state would have to take a more active role in ensuring the welfare of its society, and this meant more active state intervention in the market. Second, there was a continued commitment to some kind of liberal international economic order. Third, there was a commitment to the cooperative or multilateral management of the international economy. The result of these shared understanding among the Allies was an international economic order which attempted to develop mechanisms which would sustain some kind of international liberal order, but which would also allow both for state intervention in the domestic economy for welfarist reasons, and for cooperative management of the international economy. The resulting institutions which Ruggie discusses, the IMF and GATT, reflect this 'embedded liberalism' compromise.

Robert Latham's characterization of the post-war order as a 'liberal moment' is more ambitious (Latham 1997). He argues that the liberal order established at the end of the Second World War was a particular manifestation of 'liberal modernity'; he argues that it represented 'a historical convergence of liberalism, modernity and international order' (Latham 1997: 41). Latham understands 'liberal modernity' to consist of a number of 'domains' that are constituted by certain practices, principles, and institutions. The critical domains of liberal modernity are open international economic exchange. market orientated domestic economic relations, liberal patterns of governance, rights, and self-determination (Latham 1997: 20–33). In the post-war era these liberal 'domains' 'came to define a substantial portion of the domestic and international relations of the liberal democracies in the Atlantic Community'. These 'core' liberal states took it upon themselves in the aftermath of the Second World War to 'define relations, construct institutions, designate identities and generally organize and order a constellation of practices and principles' along liberal lines (Latham 1997: 40). The 'liberal' character of this order is found in both the substantive goals it advances and the types of interstate practices it enshrines (Latham 1997: 34–41).

There are some themes common to these characterizations of liberal order. First, there is the stress on sustaining economic openness. Second, there is the procedural norm of multilateralism and cooperation. Third, there is the recognition that this liberal order sits on certain common beliefs and commitments or a certain kind of common liberal 'identity'. Fourth, there is the stress on US hegemony and agency. The liberal order was largely made by the US, and the fact that it was the US which was hegemonic, at least for the western hemisphere, is crucial for explaining the kind of order that was created. None of these arguments pretend that the liberal order either embraced or was embraced by all states. For Deudney and Ikenberry as well as for Ruggie the liberal order they identify is clearly established in contrast to relations between the liberal core and the Soviet bloc, even if there was some desire on the part of the US to integrate the USSR and the states of Eastern Europe into this order. For Latham the international liberal order itself became defined in relation to the 'Soviet threat' (Latham 1997: 115–20).

What is less explored in these arguments is the place of newly-independent and developing countries in relation to the liberal order established by the core liberal states. The relative lack of attention paid to 'development' and developing countries is somewhat surprising because a concern with economic development was central to the aims of the liberal order. As the US State Department put it, 'this work as a whole required consideration of the political, territorial, military, economic and social conditions essential to enduring peace' (quoted in Burley 1993: 130). American planners drew the traditional liberal connection between economic prosperity and peace. To be sure, much of this was initially driven by a reflection on conditions of pre-war Europe, where it was argued that economic crisis had led directly to political violence (Latham 1997: 110–11). The concern to ensure economic prosperity was manifested in the stress on economic openness (at least within certain limits) and the establishment of a regulatory order that would ensure international economic stability. It was also given an immediate institutional embodiment in the Marshall Plan, albeit in this case yoked to an anxiety about the vulnerability of European states to communist influence. But it was also, and importantly, expressed in the establishment of the World Bank itself.

In the immediate post-war period, then, the pursuit of development became not just a moral obligation; it became wrapped up with the broader aims of the architects of the post-war order (Craig and Porter 2006: 42–8). For both of these reasons, the project of 'development' became institutionalized within international society. And, just as this has become a central norm for domestic politics so an increasingly wide range of international organisations and practices have come to express this at the international level (Ruggie 1982). These range from functional agencies such as the IMF, the WTO and the ILO to the numerous treatises and protocols designed to regulate and expand international economic activity (Onuf 1998: 156–8). The achievement of economic development has become an internationally sanctioned objective, something that these organisations *demand* of states, rather than something that simply comes from the demands placed on states by their society.

Expertise and economics

The final set of shifts within which we should locate the World Bank has to do with the rise of 'development economics' and the 'development expert'. The emergence of economics as a separate and specialized area of study consolidated the image of the economist as an expert, and economic knowledge as a specific form of expertise (Tribe 1991; Kadish and Tribe 1993; Coats 1960). The rise of 'economic expertise' was part of a more general trend in the late nineteenth and early twentieth centuries which saw 'experts' taking an increasingly significant role in public policy debates (Larson 1977; Haskell 1978). In particular, the rise of the 'expert' adviser was associated with the increasing number and complexity of the tasks facing governments, and was associated with attempts to introduce a 'neutral' and 'scientific' element into the process of government policy formulation and assessment (Critchlow 1985; Haskell 1984). A study of this significant development has argued that 'by the beginning of the twentieth century all

European societies had witnessed groups of intellectuals arguing for and pursuing empirical social research and striving to establish sciences of politics and society' (Wittrock *et al.* 1991: 35). The view that social science could contribute expert insight to the policy formulation process was based on an 'epistemological optimism' which assumed that 'methodological advances ... allowed for decisive breakthroughs in explaining and predicting social developments and, thus, achieving a cognitive mastery of society' (Wittrock *et al.* 1991: 52).

The division of economics into 'positive' and 'normative' components paved the way for the emergence of the expert economist who could assess economic policies in a 'rational' and 'scientific' manner, and whose access to economic truth (so it was argued) would transcend ideological or political debates (Benveniste 1973). As Marshall argued, 'though largely directed by practical needs, economics avoids as far as possible the discussion of those exigencies of party organization, and those diplomacies of home and foreign politics'. As a 'science' economics aims at helping the statesman decide on the ends he desires for the country and 'what are the best methods of a broad policy devoted to that end' (Marshall 1920: 36). Marshall saw the aims of economics as to 'gain knowledge for its own sake and to obtain guidance in the practical conduct of life, and especially of social life' (Marshall 1920: 36). As Mark Blaug has put it, economists were wedded to the view that it was their task 'to delineate the "possibility function", the costs and benefits of alternative allocation of scarce means; provided the means-ends distinction is rigidly maintained, economic advice to governments is, or rather can be, value free' (Blaug 1980: 129).

The image of the economist as an expert with privileged access to knowledge useful to the process of policy making was reinforced by the Keynesian revolution in economic theory and its implications for government policy making. The gradual spread of Keynesian ideas meant an expanded role for economic expertise, not only in the development of the necessary macroeconomic indicators, but also in the formulation of policies designed to guide the intensity and direction of government intervention (Wittrock *et al.* 1991: 49). Associated with this was the rapid increase in number, after the Second World War, of specialized economics research institutes (Wittrock *et al.* 1991: 48–9). In the United States, even before the influence of Keynesian ideas, social science and particularly economic 'experts' were increasingly being brought into government, most obviously under Roosevelt, but also under Hoover (Wittrock *et al.* 1991: 39). The New Deal was imbued with the idea that 'the transition to a society of abundance was a problem of engineering, not of politics' (Maier 1978: 31). This was to be accomplished rationally through technically sophisticated officials, and in a politically 'neutral' way, promoting the public interest (Burley 1993). As Maier and others have argued, this view was thoroughly implicated in the Marshall Plan, and in the international institutional arrangements put in place after the Second World War (Maier 1978).

All of these developments fed into the image and self-image of the increasing numbers of development economists:

> [To] ... the development economist belonged the expertise which was most avidly sought; it was he who knew what was needed, he who decided on the most efficient way to allocate scarce resources, he who presided over the table at which ... so many other development practitioners sat ... the economist retained for himself the ... role of giving overall directions, because it was his truth that circumscribed the task and gave it legitimacy in the name of science ... sooner or later, the Third World would yield its secrets to the gaze of the economist; and this gaze, in keeping with the best Cartesian tradition, was undeniably objective and unprejudiced.
>
> (Escobar 1995: 85)

As David Lilenthal, Director of the TVA expressed this attitude well with regard to developing countries:

> There seems to be a definite sequence in history in the change from primitive or non-industrial conditions to more highly developed modern industrial conditions. Whether all of these steps have to be taken and the intervening mistakes made is open to question ... Don't we have enough control over our destinies to short-cut those wasted steps?
>
> (Quoted in Maier 1978: 31)

The World Bank was imbued with the idea of the economist as an objective expert from its foundation. Keynes said that World Bank loans were to be used 'only for proper purposes and in proper ways, after due enquiries by experts and technicians' (quoted in Caulfield 1997: 43). Article III 5(b) of The World Bank's Articles of Agreement states that loans shall be granted with 'due attention to considerations of economy and efficiency and without regard to political or other non-economic influences or considerations'. Article IV 10 says that 'only economic considerations shall be relevant' to the Bank and its officers, and that these 'shall be weighed impartially'. Eugene Black, President of the World Bank from 1949 to 1962, said that 'the professional job of the economist is ... to make the politician [and] civil servant ... aware of the economic consequences of their decisions, and to provide evidence on which the decision-makers can weigh the benefits and costs of alternative courses of action' (Black 1963: 24). More recently, William Clausen, President of the World Bank from 1980 to 1986, said 'the bank is not a political organization, the only altar we worship at is pragmatic economics' (quoted in Hayter and Watson 1985: 196). The General Legal Council of the Bank reinforced this view when he said that, 'technical considerations of economy and efficiency rather than ideological and political considerations should guide the bank's work at all times' (Shihata 1991a: 95).

While the World Bank's operations have changed a great deal since its foundation, the idea that it possesses expert development knowledge and is in an especially privileged position to give policy advice has not changed. The most recent manifestation of this is the 1998/99 *World Development Report*, titled 'Knowledge for Development' (World Bank 1998a). The report is in part about the role that 'knowledge' can play in the development process. The Bank's view of its mission is made clear on the first page of the report: 'Knowledge is like light. Weightless and intangible, it can easily travel the world, enlightening the lives of people everywhere' (World Bank 1998a: 1). It is clear that the Bank believes that it can play a major role in dispelling darkness through the propagation of its expert knowledge. Another publication makes it clear the Bank intends to be the 'first port of call for development expertise' (World Bank 1999b: 2). The fact that the World Bank has at various times changed what it professes to 'know' about the requirements for development has not dented the institutionalized cognitive arrogance that characterizes the World Bank. It still claims to know what is best. This has remained the case even though the World Bank now also professes to be open to what 'indigenous knowledge' can contribute to development, and to be concerned to 'listen' to project beneficiaries.

The point here is not whether the World Bank really does possess expert knowledge of the problems facing developing countries, nor whether it really does know what should be done to overcome these problems. It is, rather, that the Bank's claim to be able to do these things informs its relations with its borrower countries. It is one of the factors that animated its move into new policy areas that were traditionally seen as beyond its purview. If it turned out that the Bank 'knew', for example, that a country's legal system was a significant determinant of development success, there was a prima facie case for attempting to reform legal systems through its lending.

The World Bank and economic development

The World Bank was also established as a particular kind of bank. In the Proceedings of the Bretton Woods meetings it was acknowledged that, 'the type of shareholders, the nature of its subscriptions, the exclusion of all deposits and of short-term loans, the non-profit basis, are quite foreign to the accepted nature of a Bank' (quoted in Oliver 1975: 183–4). Despite this, and despite the fact that other names were proposed for it at the Bretton Woods meetings, the World Bank was established as a bank in more than just name, and this crucially shaped the way it approached the problem of development in the years after 1945. First, and most fundamentally, the Bank was founded to provide loans for discrete development projects. Its Articles of Agreement (Article III 4(vii)) state that 'loans made or guaranteed by the Bank shall, except in special circumstances, be for the purpose of specific projects of reconstruction or development'. This clause in the Articles was to prove problematic in the early 1980s as the World Bank became involved in the provision of programme funds through its structural adjustment loans. In the early years of its operations, however, it was a guiding principle of the Bank's work and Eugene Black, President of the World Bank (1949–1963), has been quoted as saying that a loan for general purposes 'really means a loan for a purpose or purposes unknown' (quoted in Mikesell 1972: 74). The specific project approach to development was at odds with capital-centred growth theories such as those derived from the Harrod–Domar model, which informed the activities of other development agencies such as USAID (Mikesell 1972: 73, 77; Chenery and Stout 1966). In fact, this project-by-project approach to development would dog the World Bank for many years, and it is only recently that it has made comprehensive efforts to locate individual projects within larger country development plans.

Second, the World Bank was expected to raise investment capital through the sale of its own securities (bonds) in the financial markets. Though these bonds were to be guaranteed by the member governments, the Bank was nonetheless established as a financial institution with obligations to those who purchased its bonds. This crucially shaped what the Bank was able to do in its initial years of operations. When its first President, Eugene Meyer, resigned in December 1946 after only six months in the post, the Bank had sold no securities, and subsequently had very little money to lend. The new President, John McCloy brought Eugene Black with him to be the new American Executive Director and Robert Garner to be the new Vice President. All three had Wall Street banking experience and their appointment did much to raise the Bank's profile in the banking community (Caulfield 1997: 52). The problems they faced were that the Bank had very little to show for its first few months of operation, and that many bankers were still sceptical about the soundness of any prospective World Bank securities (Caulfield 1997: 49–50). McCloy, Black and Garner engaged in efforts to convince Wall Street that the Bank's securities were a sound investment and in the end the Bank's first bond issue in 1947 was heavily oversubscribed (Oliver 1975: 241). While this established a sound financial position for the Bank it also established the Bank as a 'conservative' financial institution.

The fact that the Bank was established as a particular kind of bank, and that it was run by bankers influenced its lending practices. When Chile put forward a loan request in 1946 the first President of the Bank, Eugene Meyer, said the issue was whether 'the World Bank should simply hand out money or whether it should behave as a prudent investment banker' (Mason and Asher 1972: 47). Until the establishment of IDA, the World Bank loaned money at or near market rates of interest. The rationale for World Bank lending was that as the loans were backed by capital from its member states, it was able to provide finance for projects which private investors would not provide. In the early years of its operations prospective loans were assessed using procedures followed in the private investment community. The expected values of gross benefits were compared with expected gross costs over the life of a project and the annual net benefits were compared to the proposed amount of investment (Mason and Asher 1972: 241).[2] This, combined with the rate of interest limited both the potential number of borrowers and the potential number of projects the Bank could finance. It also tended to mean that the World Bank concerned itself primarily with those domestic issues in its borrower countries that impacted upon the financial viability of proposed projects. The vast bulk of Bank lending at this time was for infrastructure projects (Mason and Asher 1972: 134, 200). The rationale for this was made clear in the Bank's *Sixth Annual Report*:

> An adequate supply of power, communications and transport facilities is a precondition for the most productive application of private savings in new enterprises. It is also the first step in the gradual industrialization and diversification of the underdeveloped countries. These basic facilities require large initial capital outlays, which, because of the low level of savings and the inadequate development of savings institutions cannot be financed wholly by the countries themselves ... Therefore the resources of the Bank are called upon to provide the foreign exchange necessary for the building of these vitally important facilities.
> (International Bank for Reconstruction and Development 1951: 14)

The primary domestic problems were seen by the Bank to be the lack of infrastructure necessary for private enterprise to flourish and the lack of domestic savings to finance infrastructural development; hence the need for World Bank loans.

Almost from the beginning of its operations the World Bank was criticized for this project-based approach to development, its stress on lending for infrastructure, and for the fact that it could not provide 'soft' loans to countries which were not in a position to borrow at market rates of interest. As early as 1949 a UN study recommended that the Bank should make loans for general development purposes, rather than for discrete projects (at least partly because of the influence of capital-growth theories) (Mikesell 1972: 73–4). Social sector lending such as that in health and education was debated within the Bank, but, at least until the 1960s was rejected on the basis that these were not sectors in which sound investments could be made and on the basis that the provision of infrastructure was the most pressing developmental task (Caulfield 1997: 63–4; Mason and Asher 1972: 152, 154). As the first official history of the World Bank put it, the Bank 'was slow to break away from its early devotion to capital infrastructure' (Mason and Asher 1972: 468). Calls for the provision of financing to developing countries on more liberal terms than that provided by the Bank started in earnest in the 1950s. The creation of IDA in 1960 was in part designed to counter these criticisms and forestall the creation of a proposed UN agency which would provide soft loans to many of the newly independent states (Mason and Asher 1972: 385). But while this agency could provide loans at much lower rates of interest it was still established as a project lending institution and project preparation was undertaken by World Bank staff.

The fact that the World Bank saw the problem of development as primarily an economic problem, and that it undertook discrete lending for mostly large-scale infrastructure projects, determined those parts of a borrower country's internal social, political, and economic arrangements the Bank considered significant in its lending. The Bank did not generally consider such matters as a country's institutional structure, the operation of its political system, or the composition of its society as important determinants of development success. Even a country's macroeconomic policy environment was not a primary target of World Bank lending.

Conclusion

The fact that the World Bank was established as a certain kind of bank and the particular way in which it understood the problem of development conditioned relations between the Bank and its borrowers up until the 1970s. Concretely they meant that the Bank did not concern itself particularly with the overall macroeconomic environment, still less the political and institutional environment, in developing countries. To be sure the Bank wanted countries to be pursuing 'sound' economic policies, but the Bank did not lend money to countries to pursue macroeconomic policy change. All this was to change in the late 1970s and into the 1980s. By 1989 the World Bank was publicly arguing that not just the macroeconomic policy environment was important, but that 'good governance' was a significant component of development success. The next chapter tells this story in detail. But it is important to note that this story unfolds within normative and institutional structures that designate the state as the vehicle for economic development on behalf of its society and that ascribes to development 'experts' a privileged cognitive position.

3 From structural adjustment to good governance

This chapter examines the expanding scope of World Bank policies in the period after 1979. During this time the Bank was led to contemplate more and more wide-ranging transformations of the economies, states, institutions, and societies of its borrower countries. The process began with the adoption of structural adjustment lending which had its theoretical grounding in neoclassical economic theory. This lending was designed to change those policies that were seen as barriers to the achievement of development success. Running alongside this was a changing view of politicians and bureaucrats. The acceptance of a New Political Economy (or Rational Choice) view of politics meant that they were increasingly depicted as essentially self-interested. Not only were the state's activities detrimental to development, but these activities were the result of the politicians and bureaucrats pursuing their personal interests at the expense of the wider economic interests of their society. These developments provided a rationale for development interventions designed to constrain the activities of the state, but the Bank still needed an account of how this was to be achieved and what exactly states should be doing to promote economic development. The latter became increasingly significant as structural adjustment lending failed to produce sustained economic growth, especially in sub-Saharan Africa. It became clear that attempting to reform and constrain the state using the 'incentives' associated with conditional lending was not working. This led the Bank to consider a much more wide-ranging institutional and political reform programme.

During this period the World Bank also became concerned with the role and significance of the 'non-state' sector. This involved the Bank beginning to contemplate the role NGOs and societal groups might play in the development process, as well as issues of participation and 'ownership'. A number of factors lay behind this, including increasingly vocal NGO criticism of the Bank, developments within the NGO sector itself, and a search for agencies other than the state that could take a role in project design and implementation. The focus on the non-state sector signalled that the composition of society and its relations with the state were significant determinants of the process of development. Finally, the growing interest in social relations within developing countries was driven by a recognition that these were important in shaping the attitudes and behaviour of individuals within society. Taken together these changes represented a massive expansion in the scope of World Bank activities. The Bank was led to consider a much broader and more far-reaching transformative project; a project that attempted to reconstruct the state, its personnel, the institutional structure necessary to sustain a market economy, and the nature of society itself. These various changes form the basis for the emergence in 1989 of a concern with 'good governance'.

In accounting for the way in which the Bank was led to contemplate this increasingly intrusive and detailed development interventions it is necessary to draw together developments and processes internal to the World Bank, as well as changes in its external environment (Stone and Wright 2007; Weaver and Leiteritz 2005). The expansion of the Bank's activities during this period is partly the result of a process of internal learning as the Bank attempted to respond to what it perceived as its previous failings. It is also the result of the Bank responding to changing external economic, political and intellectual conditions. It is only possible to understand these responses, however, by locating them within the larger international normative structure of which the Bank itself was partly a product, and which was reflected in the Bank's activities. As we argued in the last chapter there was a persistent tension between the Bank pursuing what it considered necessary to fulfil its mandate (economic development) and the constraints imposed both by the particular relationship it had with borrower governments, and more generally the norm of state sovereignty. It was during this period that this tension began to be resolved at the expense of sovereignty, largely because of a changed view of the role and nature of the state that increasingly delegitimized states' claims to sovereign statehood and non-intervention in a sphere of internal affairs.

The Berg Report and structural adjustment lending

The period from 1979 to 1981 was an important turning point in the history of the World Bank. First, in 1979, the then President of the Bank, Robert McNamara announced to the UNCTAD Conference in Manila that the Bank would undertake non-project lending for balance of payments support to those countries prepared to embrace more market-orientated economic policies. This marked the real beginning of the Bank's extensive involvement in structural adjustment lending. Second, in the same year, the African Governors of the Bank addressed a memorandum to McNamara asking the Bank to prepare a special report on the development problems facing African countries. This became known as the Berg

Report, after its principal author Elliot Berg, and was the first World Bank report to argue openly that one of the key reasons for development failure was a lack of reliance on the market mechanism to allocate economic resources (World Bank 1981). This marked the beginning of an increased acceptance within the Bank of the neoclassical counter-revolution in economics. Third, in 1979 oil prices rose for the second time in six years, and exacerbated the already difficult balance of payments situation facing many developing countries. This was an important component of the subsequent debt crisis in many developing countries, and provided an additional impetus behind the Bank's involvement in structural adjustment lending. Fourth, elections in Britain (1979) and the US (1980) returned to power politicians committed to the economic and political arguments of the new right. This marked the more general consolidation of the view that aid should be used to change what were seen as misguided economic development strategies. Finally, in 1981, a new President of the Bank (William Clausen) was appointed who actively promoted this new development agenda. There is no straightforward causal relationship between these developments. The World Bank did not pursue structural adjustment solely because there was pressure from Western governments to do so; nor was it developed solely as a response to the emerging international debt crisis. Instead, this combination of developments reinforced one another so as to produce, by the mid 1980s, an expanded role and rationale for the Bank in promoting market-orientated structural adjustment programmes.

The Bank had undertaken a small amount of non-project lending before 1979 (Mosley *et al.* 1991: 27–32). From 1963/64 until 1966, India received non-project finance for balance of payments support at the same time as the Bank was trying to persuade the Indian government to reduce the number of its trade and industrial controls and devalue the Rupee (Lipton and Toye 1990: 80–116). This was an important precedent for structural adjustment lending as it involved non-project finance to support macroeconomic policy reforms in a period of balance of payments difficulties. Nonetheless, the Bank saw such support as exceptional and by no means as an essential long-term complement to discrete project lending. The idea that such lending was to be used only in exceptional circumstances again underpinned the use of non-project finance to help a number of African countries over balance of payments difficulties created by the oil price rise of 1973 (including Kenya, Zambia and Tanzania). Such lending did, however, include a number of policy conditions including changing agricultural pricing policies and reforming state agricultural marketing boards, which would become the norm in structural adjustment lending pursued during the 1980s.

It was after the use of non-project lending in these African countries that the issue became a topic of debate within the Bank, and especially within its Board of Directors. The debates centred around five issues. First, the provision of finance to help overcome balance of payments difficulties was seen as the provenance of the IMF, and that engaging in policy-based lending would upset the already delicate demarcation of responsibilities between the two institutions (Feinberg 1988; Mosley *et al.* 1991: 3607; Polak 1994: 1501). Second, there was no explicit provision in the Bank's Articles of Agreement for large-scale non-project lending. Article III 4(vii) states that '[l]oans made or guaranteed by the Bank shall, *except in special circumstances*, be made for the *purpose of specific projects* of reconstruction or development' (emphasis added). The proviso of 'except in special circumstances' was the result of a dispute between the US and Britain during the negotiation of the Articles of Agreement. The US objected completely to the idea of non-project and stabilization loans, while Britain wanted the Bank to be able to undertake such lending to 'allow a breathing space' for the recovery of a country's economy, and to allow countries to maintain their foreign exchange balances and undertake international payments (Bitterman 1971: 68, 76). In the end the Board accepted that the Articles of Agreement did allow for the Bank to undertake non-project lending, but in keeping with the proviso of 'except in special circumstances', there was an unofficial promise on the part of the Bank's management to keep such lending to less than 10 per cent of total Bank lending. This unofficial limit did not last past the mid 1980s, however, partly because an increasing number of states were experiencing prolonged balance of payments difficulties, and partly because of a changed view of development that saw the ability of discrete project lending to contribute to development as dependent on the policy reforms structural adjustment lending was designed to achieve.

Third, there were doubts expressed, both on the Board – and in the Bank more generally – about whether the World Bank really had the necessary expertise in this area. At the time the Bank had relatively few general macroeconomists (Stern 1991: 3). Most Bank economists were sector specialists or worked in the finance and assessment departments. This chimed with worries over the demarcation of responsibilities with the IMF, which traditionally had a much stronger general macroeconomic focus. Fourth, there were doubts expressed about the usefulness of non-project lending as an instrument for changing recipient economic policies. Certainly there were those within the Bank who were becoming disillusioned with the ability of dialogue alone to induce policy change, but equally there were doubts expressed about the willingness of recipient countries to change bad policies for good; and if they were already committed to better policies there was no need for conditional lending (Mosley *et al.* 1991: 33). This was to become a central issue during the 1980s as it became clear that there were severe limits to the Bank's ability to exercise leverage over its borrowers. Finally, there were worries within the Board of Directors about the extent to which the Bank should (as opposed to could) use its financial leverage to induce macroeconomic policy change. This was seen by some Board members, particularly those representing the Bank's borrowers, as unwarranted meddling in internal affairs and potentially damaging to the Bank's reputation for political neutrality (Mosley *et al.* 1991: 35–6). It is clear that many board members recognized that this type of lending would lead to increasingly intrusive development interventions that threatened the traditional relationship between the Bank and its borrower governments.

It was in the context of this set of internal debates about the World Bank's role in policy-based lending that the Berg Report was researched and written. The report highlighted what it saw as a developing economic crisis in sub-Saharan Africa. It pinpointed slow overall economic growth coupled with rapid population growth, very sluggish growth in agriculture and increasing balance of payments and fiscal crises leading to a rapid rise in external indebtedness (World Bank 1981: 2–4). The report argued that this emerging crisis was due to three factors. First, there were certain basic constraints on economic development such as underdeveloped human resources, climatic and geographical factors, and rapid population growth. Second, changes in the external economic environment, including recession in the developed world, oil price rises, and adverse terms of trade for primary products in general. Third, what the report called 'domestic policy inadequacies'. These included trade and exchange rate policies, pricing and taxation policies in the agricultural sector, and an over-reliance on the government for resource mobilization and allocation, especially 'given the widespread weakness of planning, decision making and management' within many African governments (World Bank 1981: 4). While the report identified three causes of economic crisis in Africa, it concentrated on the last of them in its analysis of what African governments and aid donors should do to stimulate growth.

The recommendations of the report derive from basic neoclassical economic theory. The focus was on the perceived need to restructure the incentives facing particularly agricultural producers. First, it argued there was a need to liberalize trade and exchange rate controls to create incentives for agricultural producers to engage in the production of exports crops. Second, it argued there was a need to raise producer prices and rely on the market mechanism rather than state agricultural marketing boards to allocate agricultural resources. Underpinning these recommendations was the view that agricultural producers were rational economic agents: 'all the evidence points to the fact that smallholders are outstanding managers of their own resources ... [and] can be counted on to respond to changes in the profitability of different crops and of other farming activities' (World Bank 1981: 4). Beyond the focus on agricultural production, the report argued that African governments had relied too little on the market to allocate economic resources, and that African governments were too big and too inefficient. Finally, the Berg Report signalled the importance of non-project financing in assisting African countries to undertake 'major changes in policies'. It argued that while project lending would remain the dominant vehicle of resource transfer to Africa, 'the formulation of sound projects ... should increasingly be within an agreed policy framework' (World Bank 1981: 30, 50–68, 35–44, 125–7).[1]

The Berg Report was heavily criticized both inside the Bank at the prepublication stage, and outside the Bank when the report was published in 1981. Within the Bank, the report was seen as a criticism of the majority of Bank operations in Africa, which were still based on financing discrete development projects. In addition, the strongly market-orientated message of the report upset many within the Bank who remained committed to large scale capital flows to African countries, and to the explicit poverty reduction and redistribution focus of much of the Banks high profile work in the 1970s (Chenery *et al.* 1974). Despite these criticisms, the report was passed by the Board, even though there is no doubt that its message was unpopular with many of its members. There were at least five reasons for this.

First, it is significant that Elliot Berg was appointed to write the report by Ernest Stern. There seems to be a consensus among commentators and World Bank staff that Ernest Stern was the most influential individual within the Bank from the time he became Vice President for Operations in 1978 until his retirement in 1994. Bruce Rich has said that, 'it was obvious to many that Stern, with his encyclopedic knowledge of the Bank's unwritten history and rules, and his powerful web of internal contacts and allies, was the man who really ran the place' (Rich 1994: 126). Stern remained a fierce advocate of the report, and at prepublication meetings where it was discussed he is reported to have effectively sidelined those who did not agree with the report's findings.[2] Second, the new World Bank President, A. W. Clausen, supported the report which was more in line with his own views about the role of markets and the private sector. In 1982 Clausen said that 'those countries that have demonstrated the best economic performance have encouraged the private sector'. This he said was not surprising, 'because it means they have simply encouraged a human characteristic that is universal ... the entrepreneurial energy latent in their own citizenry' (Clausen 1982: 68; World Bank 1986b). Third, the appointment of Clausen led to the resignation of a number of the more high-profile internal critics of the report and of the neoclassical approach to development more generally (Ayers 1983: 230). Fourth, the US and British Executive Directors were backed by governments who strongly endorsed the message of the report (Ayers 1983: 231; Howe 1982). In the early 1980s the US held about 22 per cent of the votes on the Board and Britain about another 7 per cent, and all Bank reports are approved by a simple majority. One final reason for the Board's acceptance of the report was that the Board itself had rarely overturned recommendations from the Bank's senior management during McNamara's years as president (McKitterick 1986). So, despite serious criticisms of the report it became the basis for a new Bank strategy for African development.

Before considering the consolidation of the neoclassical view of development within the Bank and the associated rise in policy-based lending, it is worth pausing to consider the view of the economy represented by the Berg Report and the barriers the report identified to economic development. It is clear that the report viewed the main obstacle to development in sub-Saharan Africa to have been government interference in the operation of the market. To be sure the report also recognized that changing external economic conditions had contributed to Africa's economic malaise, but the way forward was to be a reduction in government control of the economy. As has been argued, underlying this was a faith in the economic rationality of consumers and producers who, through the operation of the market, would produce an efficient allocation of resources and a dynamic economy. In this view the dynamism of the market economy was simply waiting to be 'released' from the constraints of government. Despite the controversial arguments of the report, this was in fact a very simple message.

Adjustment lending, neoclassical economics and the 'new political economy'

During the early 1980s structural adjustment loans were large, fast disbursing, and typically had many policy conditions attached to them. The conditions attached to a loan were spread over a number of areas and typically included the removal of import quotas, cutting tariffs, reducing interest rate controls, removal of agricultural price controls, elimination of state marketing boards, removal of restrictions on industry, improving the management of state owned enterprises, and removal of price controls on food, energy, and agricultural inputs. There was a dramatic expansion of adjustment lending during this period, and by the end of the decade adjustment lending accounted for over a quarter of all Bank lending commitments (Table 3.1). Investment lending still comprised the bulk of Bank lending, but the success of project lending came to be seen as increasingly dependent on the success of macroeconomic adjustment.

One impetus behind the expansion of structural adjustment lending was the debt crisis (Bergesen and Lunde 1999: 129–30). The rising external debt of many developing countries had been a concern within the Bank for some years, but the attention given to it tended to concentrate on the problems this posed for the debtor countries themselves. During the late 1970s and early 1980s the rapid rise of external debt under the triple impact of rising oil prices, rising real dollar interest rates and worldwide economic downturn came to be seen as a more general threat to the international financial system and Western commercial banks (Helleiner 1980: 107–10). This culminated in 1983, when a number of Latin American debtors were unable or unwilling to service their external debts. Even though the external debt of some Latin American countries, particularly Mexico, Brazil and Argentina, may have posed a threat to Western banks, it is clear that by this time the use of structural adjustment loans was seen by the World Bank as an essential first step towards renewed economic growth and not simply as a way of ensuring the repayment of loans made by private banks. The debt crisis in large part ended the debate within the Bank over whether or not it should undertake policy-based lending. There remained many external critics of the programmes, and there were Bank staff who had reservations about particular policy conditions, or particular loans; but the combination of the debt crisis and a new understanding of the barriers to development success ensured the Bank remained committed to using its lending to alter recipient economic policies.

During the second half of the 1980s the Bank turned increasingly toward the use of sectoral adjustment loans (SECAL) rather than more general structural adjustment loans (Table 3.2). SECALs were designed to pursue the objective of economic policy reform at a sectoral rather than economy-wide level, and as such they usually involved smaller amounts of money and tended to have had fewer conditions attached to them. This made them

Table 3.1 World Bank Commitments by Lending Instrument (annual average percentage shares) 1976–1990

	FY1976–80	*FY1981–85*	*FY1986–90*
Specific projects	56	45	46
Financial intermediary loans	17	16	10
Sectoral investment loans	21	25	16
Other investment loans	1	2	3
Total investment lending	95	88	74
Adjustment lending	5	12	26

Source: World Bank

easier for the Bank to implement and monitor, and they could be undertaken in countries when the Bank and the borrower government could not agree on an overall programme of macroeconomic policy changes. Most important of all, SECALs proved to be a more effective instrument for the pursuit of economic restructuring (Jayarajah and Branson 1995: 108–9). The World Bank remained committed to using non-project finance to induce economic policy change, but it was increasingly targeting this lending at specific sectors of an economy, rather than at the economy as a whole.

Running alongside the expansion of structural and sectoral adjustment lending, the Bank undertook a large amount of research into the theoretical and practical issues raised by the Berg Report. The report itself had only provided the most general theoretical justification for a move towards an increased reliance on the market mechanism in development. In order to operationalize this effectively more research was needed on the problems facing specific sectors of the economy, on the timing and sequencing of reforms, and perhaps above all on the 'political economy' of reform. The Berg Report had not really tackled this latter issue, and the Bank had little understanding of the social and political obstacles to structural adjustment. These new intellectual challenges necessitated a change in both the composition of the research arm of the Bank and a change in the focus of its research.

An important sign of the increased significance of neoclassical economics for the Bank during this period was the appointment in 1982 of Anne O. Krueger as Vice President for Economics and Research. She replaced Hollis Chenery who had been the leader of the major Bank research effort of the 1970s, *Redistribution with Growth*, and who had been a pioneer in the field of 'development economics' (Chenery *et al.* 1974). In line with the concerns of Development Economics in the 1960s and 1970s, Chenery had emphasized the importance of overcoming internal structural bottlenecks through increased capital flows (Chenery 1975). Krueger had a quite different understanding of the process of economic development. In an article published in 1986, while still Vice President for Economics and Research, Krueger systematically criticized what she understood as

Table 3.2 World Bank SAL and SECAL commitments (annual average percentage share) 1976–1990

Loan category	FY1976–80	FY1981–85	FY1986–90
Total adjustment lending	5	12	26
SALs	4	7	7
SECALs	1	5	18

Source: World Bank

'orthodox' development economics including the early work of Hollis Chenery (Krueger 1986). In that article she cited the work of T. W. Schultz who argued that peasant producers were 'rational but poor'; that is, they responded to economic incentives in the way predicted by neoclassical economics (Schultz 1964). She also argued that the emphasis on capital flows in orthodox development economics was mistaken, and that market incentives and outward orientated trade policies were much more important determinants of economic growth (Krueger 1986: 197). By the middle of the 1980s these views had become increasingly dominant in the research arm of the Bank. In 1985, *The World Bank Research News* said that,

> [t]he record of development and the growing store of empirical research have heightened recognition of the importance of markets and incentives – and of the limits of government intervention and planning. The new vision of growth is that markets and incentives can work in developing countries ... physical investment is only one determinant of the speed of development ... [and] the economic policies of governments, and the distortions they induce, are now a major focus of the analysis of development policy.
>
> (World Bank 1985: 1)

As neoclassical economics became more dominant within the Bank, so the issue of the political and institutional barriers to adjustment became more significant. In her 1986 article, Krueger signalled a general theoretical framework for approaching these problems. Krueger had been a pioneer in the field of applying new political economy to understanding the behaviour of politicians and bureaucrats (Krueger 1974). There was, she said, an 'increased recognition that bureaucrats and others develop a vested interest in [economic] controls', and that, 'even if they originally have a positive impact on welfare, [economic controls] may over time have increased costs both because constituencies build up seeking yet further policy interventions and because political resistance to change increases' (Krueger 1986: 201). A growing concern with the political economy of government controls and economic policy change can be seen in a number of other papers and research projects during this time (Krueger *et al.* 1991/92). The move towards a New Political Economy approach to analyzing politics can also be seen in the work of Deepak Lal who worked in the research department from 1984 to 1986.[3] While at the Bank he systematically criticized the assumption that governments are 'benevolent and well-informed' (Lal 1984). He argued that,

> for many developing countries in the past three decades, a vast expansion of the government bureaucracy, of the public sector, and of

controls on industry, prices, and foreign trade have created a new system of subinfeudalization, in which politically created property rights to rents for various groups are financed by implicit or explicit taxation of the general population.

It was this situation, so he argued, which provided the 'strongest political and practical case for the promotion of a market economy' (Lal 1987: 293).

Not all World Bank staff agreed with these arguments, and many Bank staff continued their sector-specific project preparation and research without considering them. But it is clear that by the mid 1980s there had been a change in the Bank's official intellectual model, and in its understanding of the role and nature of the state. The Bank's 1988 *Annual Report* argued that 'individuals whether in or out of government use the resources at their disposal to further their own private interests' (World Bank 1988: 49–51). There is little doubt, as one commentator has argued, that the Bank was 'strongly influenced' by this approach to understanding political economy (Toye 1992: 184). Despite the fact that these views were not shared by all Bank staff, they became significant because of the new place which structural adjustment lending occupied within the Bank. Increasingly it became accepted that the success of discrete project lending depended upon successful adjustment of economic policies, and this in turn depended upon the ability of the Bank to understand and explain the activities of politicians and bureaucrats who had continued to implement what were seen as 'irrational' economic policies.

The acceptance of a new political economy approach to understanding the political and social obstacles to economic policy change had a very significant implication for the notion of state sovereignty and the idea of 'internal affairs'. Governments, politicians and bureaucrats were no longer seen as simply mistaken about economic policy, or inexperienced, or the victims of unfortunate international economic circumstances; rather they were themselves a major cause of economic decline. Once this had become accepted, the relationship between the state and its economy and society was conceived as fundamentally antagonistic; as a clash of interests in which the more powerful politicians and bureaucrats were wining out to the economic detriment of much of the rest of the population. Craig and Porter put this view as that of 'bad policemen and greedy officials, abusing power to oppress the poor' (Craig and Porter 2006: 8). Seen in this way, these arguments provided a powerful justification for increasingly intrusive development strategies; for in any developmental accounting the real economic interests of society would take preference over the detrimental actions of a small number of self-seeking politicians and bureaucrats (Hawthorn and Seabright 1993). World Bank lending was predicated on the belief that structural adjustment would be good for the populace of developing countries, at least in the longer run. The Bank not only claimed to know better than developing country governments about what was good for their economies and societies, it also argued that these governments were actively damaging the economic well-being of their populace; and this justified increasing intervention in the process of economic policy making that had traditionally been seen as a sphere of internal affairs.

Problems with structural adjustment

None of this resolved the practical problems of engaging in more intrusive development strategies, especially as the Bank was constrained by its Articles of Agreement to lend only to governments or when governments have guaranteed repayment of the loan. The original tool for inducing policy change was conditional lending. It became increasingly clear, however, that conditional lending was not a very effective tool of policy change. One analysis has shown that during the 1980s, only 55 per cent of World Bank policy conditions were ever implemented by developing countries. In some countries which received structural adjustment loans this was as low as 15 per cent (Mosley *et al.* 1991: 136). On the Bank's own analysis of the motivations of politicians and bureaucrats, the reluctance to implement loan conditions is unsurprising. Politicians, bureaucrats and societal groups have a vested interest in maintaining the policy status quo because there are political and economic benefits from doing so, and if politicians rely on these societal groups for continued political support then there is a strong disincentive to engage in policy reform. In principle the incentives facing politicians and bureaucrats were to be countered by the incentives provided by conditional lending: more lending if governments implemented policy changes, less lending if they did not. In practice, however, policy-based lending did not work like this.

First, structural adjustment loans were disbursed in tranches (World Bank 1992a: ch. 3). In order for the first tranche of a loan to be disbursed, the borrower government had to commit itself to undertaking reforms, but the first tranche was normally disbursed before any reforms had been completed. This meant that it was only with the second tranche that the Bank could use its financial leverage to ensure compliance. At this stage it was possible for the borrower government to use a number of tactics to ensure continued disbursement, while not fully implementing loan conditions. During the 1980s there seem to have been only two cases when the second tranche of a structural adjustment loan was not disbursed, despite there being obvious problems of implementation in many other cases (Mosley *et al.*

1991: 166). Second, the amount of leverage the Bank was able to exert depended in part on the borrower government's access to alternative sources of capital. The availability of other sources of finance enabled certain borrower governments, especially those in middle-income countries, to avoid implementing World Bank loan conditions. Third, the Bank had few mechanisms for ensuring that policy changes were maintained once the loan has been fully disbursed, and borrower governments often had strong incentives to revert to their original policies. Fourth, governments that did not implement loan conditions would almost certainly have access to more adjustment loans at a later date. This is partly because the Bank believed that macroeconomic adjustment was desirable and that it should assist countries wherever possible to undertake it, but it is also linked to what has been called the 'lending culture' of the Bank. Traditionally, promotion to senior positions within the Bank in part depended on the amount of money which staffers loaned (Naim 1994). Structural adjustment loans allowed staff members to engage in large, high profile lending, and in a situation such as this Bank staff had good reasons to undertake lending to governments which had a poor record of loan implementation. So, for example, countries such as the Central African Republic, Côte d'Ivoire, Jamaica, Kenya, the Philippines, Uruguay, and Zaire all received structural adjustment loans, even when a previous structural adjustment loan was deemed, on the Bank's own terms, to have been 'unsatisfactory' (Johnson and Wasty 1993).

What all of this showed was that attempting to use incentives as a mechanism for inducing policy reform was less than successful. It was this that led to a crucial reworking of the strategy for pursuing economic reforms. The Bank had the most success with implementation of its loan conditions in those countries where governments were already committed to pursuing a reform programme (although even here the implementation rate was less then 100 per cent). The recognition that successful implementation of structural adjustment required government commitment led the Bank to recognize the importance of the 'borrower ownership' of adjustment programmes (Johnson and Wasty 1993). It also led them to realize the importance of strategies to *generate* this 'ownership' both within borrower governments and within societal groups. That is, because of the limited leverage which the Bank's finance provided in the face of entrenched interests, the Bank began to search for ways not of ensuring compliance, but of *ensuring agreement* with its loans conditions, and this has been pursued through extensive 'dialogue', 'participation' in programme design, and a programme of education and training for government officials (Hodd 1987). The Bank could not simply 'fight fire with fire' in the sense of using its finance to counter vested political interests. Rather, it had to find ways to rework the attitudes and commitments of politicians and bureaucrats.

Beyond the problem of implementation, another very significant problem with policy-based lending was becoming apparent. It was becoming increasingly clear that even when short-term macroeconomic balance had been achieved, the supply-side response of adjusting economies was much, much slower (World Bank 1993b). The expected improvements in investment, productivity and output were in many cases so slow in coming that they potentially endangered the whole adjustment effort as neither interest groups nor politicians would receive substantial benefits in the short or even medium term from structural adjustment (Mosley *et al.* 1991: chs 6, 7 and 8). The Bank began to argue that a major reason for the poor private sector response to adjustment, especially in the non-export sector, was the institutional framework within which the private sector operated. This led the Bank beyond the issue of unnecessary government regulation of the economy to such issues as the legal system, the regulatory framework, contract enforcement, the predictability of government policy, the banking and financial systems, and the lack of accurate and timely economic information (Paul 1987c). This implied that much more detailed institutional engineering was necessary to produce a dynamic market economy.

Institutions matter

For a long time the World Bank had included a certain amount of 'institutional development' (ID) work in its lending, either integrated into projects or as free-standing Technical Assistance (TA). During the early 1980s the Bank began to concern itself with what it called 'public sector management' issues and their impact on the ability to undertake structural adjustment lending. The first attempt to systematically detail the importance of institutional issues in the context of structural adjustment lending came in the 1983 *World Development Report* (World Bank 1983a). This report reaffirmed the Bank's commitment to reforming economic policy and reducing the role of the state in resource allocation (World Bank 1983a: ch. 5). But it also recognized that 'bureaucratic failing', in the form of corruption, lack of 'capacity', lack of coordination and lack of consultation, were critical impediments to developmental success (World Bank 1983a: 94, 64–70). The report had three significant things to say about how these problems were to be overcome.

First, it noted how the development of effective public administrations in developed countries (Britain, US and Japan) was prompted by 'the growth of national economies and the rapid development of markets' (World Bank 1983a: 116). This left the relationship between effective public administration and economic growth rather opaque, but it did hint at the pressures which could be brought to bear on governments by the economic and social groups thought to be produced by a vibrant market economy, and in so doing it fore-shadowed the Bank's concern with the role of 'civil society' in the development of 'good governance'. Second, the report stressed that 'strong and effective public institutions' were necessary for development, but argued that such institutions must be ones which 'best fit the societies they are intended to serve' (World Bank 1983a: 115). Again, quite what this entailed was not made clear, but it did suggest that the Bank was going to have to know a great deal more about these societies if it was to pursue institutional reform. Third, the report's specific prescriptions for institutional reform recognized that more thoroughgoing institutional reform required above all that 'public enterprises and bureaucracies [become] more responsive to their ministries and their clientele, and ... achieve a closer connection between inputs and outputs' (World Bank 1983a: 117–20, 123). The report argued that making public institutions more 'responsive' and more efficient could be achieved through the use of 'market surrogate' strategies such as various forms of decentralization, increasing the accountability of individuals within bureaucracies and the marketization of relationships within the public sector.

This report provided the impetus behind the much increased attention given to institutional issues in the following years. In 1984 a report on sub-Saharan Africa noted a 'systematic weakness in African governmental institutions' (World Bank 1984: 39). The Bank's education and training department, the Economic Development Institute (EDI) was brought within the operations complex of the Bank in 1985 and charged with 'building country capabilities for economic management' (De Lusignan 1986). EDI organized increasing numbers of training courses and seminars for bureaucrats in developing countries, and increasing amounts of training directed at specific ministries (Table 3.3).

A large number of research projects and working papers were produced on issues such as macroeconomic management, public administration and institutional issues in development (Lamb and Muller 1982; Rhee 1985; Lamb 1987). There were also a number of attempts to detail more precisely what kinds of market-surrogate approaches were possible in institutional reform. These focused on the possibility of introducing incentives to improve bureaucratic performance, such as improved status, increasing perks and pay, increased use of audits and assessments, increased competition within and between institutions, exposure to 'market discipline', and the introduction of 'voice' and 'exit' options for beneficiaries and clients (Israel 1987; Paul 1991, 1992).

What is significant about these strategies of institutional reform is that they require that the day-to-day workings of individual bureaucrats, as well as entire bureaucracies, and their relations with politicians and clients, be brought into view. That is, they require for their implementation a greatly

Table 3.3 EDI Teaching and Institutional Assistance Programs 1984–1989

Year	1984	1985	1986	1987	1988	1989
No. of activities	86	124	151	167	195	209

Source: World Bank

increased surveillance capacity on the part of the Bank, and much more precisely targeted reform packages. This sort of approach to institutional reform is an important step along the road towards the Bank's concern with transforming the attitudes, habits and patterns of thought and conduct of individuals and groups in developing countries. The Bank was led to this through recognition that these factors were important in determining the performance of institutions, which were themselves important in determining the success of structural adjustment as well as discrete project lending.

The actual practice of ID within Bank lending was slow to match this proliferation of conceptual research. It was only in the 1990s that the amount of lending for TA started to rise dramatically (Paul 1990: 4, 35; C. Gray *et al.* 1990; Brinkerhoff 1994). In addition, the ID/TA components of Bank loans often failed to achieve their stated objectives. An Operations Evaluation Department (OED) study showed that less than one third of all Bank projects assessed 'substantially achieved' their ID objectives (World Bank 1994b: 132). Another OED survey indicated that the Bank's record in assisting African ID had been 'poor' (World Bank 1990c). Even in the core area of civil service reform, where the Bank undertook 55 operations between 1981 and 1988, the Bank's record was poor, and the reforms tended to concentrate on cost containment and rationalization of remuneration, rather than pursuing a 'coherent, overarching strategy' of institutional development (Nunberg and Nellis 1995: 5–8, 43). There were at least three reasons for this. First, staff were wary of ID work because the Bank had relatively little knowledge about ID issues, and as such seemed too unspecific to be systematically integrated into lending. Second, there were continued pressures on Bank staff to design and get projects approved quickly which reduced the time available for developing sophisticated and subtle ID/PSM components (Naim 1994). Third, there remained an unresolved tension between the research and operations arms of the Bank. The Bank's research arm has always prided itself on producing high quality and cutting edge research which had a reputation among operational staff for not being directly operationally usable. During this period, the extent to which the more innovative ID/PSM proposals were taken seriously in lending depended largely on the particular task manager's own experiences and educational background (C. Gray *et al.* 1990).

Significantly, though, the Bank's Operations Evaluation Department (OED) continually insisted on the importance of institutional development for project and programme success. OED was formally independent of the rest of the Bank and reported directly to the Board of Directors. Each OED report was the product of a fairly sophisticated cost-benefit evaluation methodology, and the Banks management had to respond formally to each report (Carlsson *et al.* 1994: chs 2 and 7). In numerous evaluations of the Bank's lending, OED argued that a key factor determining success was the extent and quality of ID; and this applied to both project and adjustment lending (World Bank 1994b, 1995a; Jayarajah and Branson 1995). It was increasingly difficult for the Board and the Bank's management to ignore the findings of these reports, and they led to the introduction of mechanisms to ensure lessons learned from OED evaluations were taken into account in the design of projects and programmes.

The Bank's experience with institutional development issues in the 1980s demonstrates the difficulties the Bank had in effectively integrating new sets of issues into its lending. The rationale for an increased concern with institutional development became firmly established, and the Bank's evaluations of its lending demonstrated that if it was to be successful institutional development was going to have to be accorded a much higher profile. The trouble was that this took some time to filter down to staff in lending departments. By the mid 1990s this process was much further on, and as these issues became more accepted, so more and more of the Bank's work involved detailed attempts to reform civil services, civil servants themselves, and to construct in a detailed way the institutional foundations of a market economy.

The 'non-state' sector

The final significant development in World Bank policies during this period was the increased attention being paid to issues such as the participation of project beneficiaries and stakeholders, 'indigenous' peoples, and the role of NGOs. By the early 1990s these concerns had fed into other new areas such as increased attention to the idea of 'culture'.[4] As the Bank expanded its interest in these areas, so it was drawn into activities that targeted not just the state and its personnel, but the composition of society itself, and the attitudes, habits and mores of individuals. This focus completed the 'model' the Bank was attempting to implement. This now included a market based economy, an effective and efficient administrative structure, a comprehensive institutional structure designed to facilitate the market economy, and a vibrant 'civil society' composed of the 'appropriate' social groups exhibiting the 'right' kinds of attitudes.

Concern about the participation of groups affected by Bank projects, especially 'indigenous groups', and co-operation with NGOs, were not wholly new issues for the Bank. In 1981 the Bank issued guidelines on project appraisal which recognized the need to 'elicit and sustain beneficiary participation', and as early as 1984, the Bank was publishing evidence about the beneficial impact of local participation in the design and implementation of Bank projects (Paul 1987b; Cernea 1984). The first explicit recognition of the needs of 'indigenous' peoples came in 1982 when an 'Operational Manual Statement' was issued to staff which recognized that 'special measures' were needed to protect tribal peoples from the harmful effects of development projects and promised that 'as a general policy' the Bank would not assist development projects that led to undesirable effects on tribal peoples, unless adequate safeguards were provided (World Bank 1982; Davis 1993; A. Gray 1998). Co-operation with various NGOs, particularly as project advisers and implementing agencies, had been under way on a small scale since 1973, and in 1981 a NGO–World Bank committee was established to provide a permanent forum for discussion (Salmen and Eaves 1991). In the same year an 'Operational Policy Note' was issued to staff which gave guidelines for staff on NGO involvement in project design. finance and implementation, and in 1983 an 'Adviser on Intergovernmental and Non-Governmental Organisations' was appointed (Shihata 1992: 624–5). Despite this, through the early 1980s these remained fairly peripheral issues especially when it came to actual lending. There were two important developments that brought them to the fore.

First, the Bank's record on the environment, participation and indigenous peoples came under sustained attack from NGOs and the US Congress during the 1980s (Wade 2004). NGO criticism centred around what they saw as the adverse effects of structural adjustment on the poorest groups in society, and on the Bank's record on environmental protection and indigenous groups (Clark 1991; NGO Working Group on the World Bank 1989). In 1983, environmental groups persuaded the House Subcommittee on International Development Institutions and Finance to hold oversight hearings on the Multilateral Development Banks (MDBs) and the environment (Rich 1994: ch. 5; Le Pestre 1989: ch. 3). In December 1984, the committee issued a series of recommendations which included increasing the number of environmental staff at the Bank, increasing the number of smaller-scale, environmentally beneficial projects, and sharing information with NGOs (Rich 1994: 210–12). Alongside these general pressures were increasingly high profile campaigns about a number of Bank projects, especially the Polonoroeste and Sardar Sarovar (Narmada Dam) projects. In these cases the Bank was financing large scale, potentially environmentally damaging projects which displaced thousands of indigenous and other persons without 'adequate safeguards' (Rich 1994: 121). Critics accused the Bank of not following its own guidelines on the protection of indigenous peoples and environmental assessment and of not consulting those most affected by the projects. These campaigns also involved pressure on the Bank's Executive Directors, and the US, German, Dutch, Australian and Swedish Executive Directors, among others, pressured the Bank's management for action. In 1985 the Bank stopped disbursements on the Polonoroeste project pending the introduction of increased environmental protection measures, and the Bank was pressured to redesign a proposed dam project in the Amazon basin (Rich 1994: 136–8). In response to this pressure, the Bank drew up a new series of environmental protection measures in 1987, which included the establishment of a new environmental department and individual country environmental assessments (Le Pestre 1989: 199–201). Critics charged (and still charge) that the Bank has not done enough, that it does not follow its own guidelines, and that, at the extreme, the Bank's entire development vision is not compatible with effective environmental protection (Wade 2004). What is important here is that these campaigns brought issues of NGO cooperation, information sharing and stakeholder participation to the fore, both within and outside the Bank.

Second, during the 1980s the role of developmental NGOs in general was changing. The number of NGOs and the scale of their operations increased dramatically. According to one source, the number of development NGOs based in OECD countries rose from 1,702 in 1981 to 2,542 in 1990, and it has been estimated that there were over 6,000 worldwide by 1989 (Charities Aid Foundation 1991; Bratton 1989). Private grants to NGOs rose from US$2,386 million in 1980, to US$4,224 million in 1988, and by the end of the decade NGOs accounted for 12.9 per cent of all overseas development assistance (Charities Aid Foundation 1991: 154). Many Western NGOs expanded their work beyond disaster and emergency relief into broader development activities, and NGOs increasingly accepted funding from donor governments. To date, Germany, Sweden, Australia, The Netherlands, Norway, Britain, France, the US and the European Union, all have co-financing arrangements with NGOs, and the total amount of official funding for NGOs in OECD countries rose by 55 per cent between 1980 and 1988 (Burnell 1991: 211; Charities Aid Foundation: 154). In Britain, the Joint Funding Scheme channelled £16 million to NGOs in 1989/90, up from £2 million in 1980/81. The increase in official funding created dilemmas for NGOs, not least of which is the fact that it may compromise their ability to criticize official aid policy, and it has also increased the pressure on them to introduce more rigorous monitoring and evaluation procedures and opened them up to an examination of their performance and accountability (Robinson 1991; OECD 1988; Brett 1993). These developments, however, gave NGOs an increasingly high profile role in development generally, and especially on the agendas of official donors.

This general pattern of changes in the NGO sector and relations between NGOs and official donors was mirrored in the work of the World Bank. In September 1988 the then President of the Bank, Barber Conable, said that 'NGOs ... have enormous potential for flexible and effective action. I have encouraged Bank staff to initiate a broadened dialogue with NGOs' (World Bank 1990c: 69). In the same year the Bank published its first attempt to outline the role of NGOs in development (Cernea 1988). In 1989 the Bank issued an Operational Directive on collaboration with NGOs which set out their potential role in project identification, design, financing, implementation and evaluation. There then followed a large number of publications dealing with NGOs and community groups, which culminated in a 'Sourcebook' for Bank staff (World Bank 1990b; Hussi *et al.* 1993; Stevaluk and Thompson 1993; World Bank 1994c). World Bank collaboration with NGOs increased dramatically from around 20 per cent of projects in 1989 to 50 per cent in FY 1994 (World Bank 1995c). The Bank also increased its collaboration with grass-roots and indigenous groups as well as large Western NGOs. Of these collaborations by far the largest number, 90 per cent, involved NGOs as implementing agencies, 50 per cent in project design and between 10 and 20 per cent in co-financing arrangements. In FY 1994, 32 per cent of these projects were in rural development, 21 per cent in infrastructure and urban development and 10 per cent were adjustment related (World Bank 1995c).

Increased cooperation with NGOs led in turn to an increased attention to the issue of 'participation'. Pressure for the Bank to recognize the importance of participation by beneficiaries or 'stakeholders' culminated in 1990 with the establishment of a Bank-wide 'Learning Group' on popular participation, supported by two Bank Vice Presidents (Paul 1987b; Salmen 1987; Bhatnagar and Williams 1992a). A core team was given a mandate to develop and document Bank operations that were considered participatory and then to recommend changes in Bank operations. This process was given added impetus by OED evidence that there was a correlation between the level of beneficiary participation and 'ownership' and project success (World Bank 1994b, 1995a). In addition it was becoming clear that 'ownership' of adjustment programmes was important for their success and that it was vital to involve local people in environmental protection schemes (Johnson and Wasty 1993).

Neither collaboration with NGOs nor beneficiary/stakeholder participation permeated everywhere in the Bank. The extent to which they were integrated into lending partly depended on the attitudes of particular task managers as well as on the different development priorities in different regions. Indeed, there were a number of specific difficulties for the Bank in both these areas. First, for all the emphasis on the role of the market and the importance of the non-state sector, it is committed to working with recipient governments. Governments remain the guarantors of Bank loans, and the extent of participation and collaboration with NGOs depends to an important extent on the goodwill of governments or the pressure the Bank can bring to bear on these governments (Bratton 1989; Fowler 1993). Without government support there is little the Bank can do to initiate, broaden and sustain participation and NGO collaboration. According to the World Bank Sourcebook on participation, if a government 'adamantly' opposes the use of a participatory process, the choice for the Task Manager is either to withdraw from the project, or wait for the right moment to exert pressure again (World Bank 1994c; Sandstrom 1994). There were also a number of problems associated with the internal culture of the Bank. The use of beneficiary participation and NGO collaboration make projects more complicated, and extend the time necessary for project preparation. There is still a feeling within the Bank that the 'lending culture' has not been completely transcended and, at least until very recently, a feeling that there were few rewards for staff undertaking innovative approaches to loan preparation (Crawford 1992).

Despite these difficulties NGO cooperation and beneficiary 'participation' became increasingly important all through the 1990s, culminating in the PRSP process. First, both are related to the general reconfiguration of the role of the state in development. Structural adjustment and the analysis of the role and operations of the state and its civil servants provided a rationale for a reduction in the role of the state as a direct service provider. This, combined with the increasing fiscal pressures on governments, led to a search for alternative service providers in areas such as health, agriculture and education, where outright market provision is either impossible or politically very difficult. Second, they are linked to the Bank's understanding of the need for institutional reform. It has been argued within the Bank that one of the mechanisms for improving institutional performance is to make institutions more accountable to their 'stakeholders'. NGOs and other grassroots organizations can in some instances pressure institutions for better performance. The concern with NGOs, community groups and participation should be understood as part of a concern to both restructure society and restructure the relations between the state and society. Third, and most importantly, both of these issues are related to an explicit recognition on the part of the Bank of the need for changes in the attitudes, habits and mores of individuals in society.

In areas requiring *changes in individual and household behaviour* – like family planning, savings and credit, income generation, and the adoption of new farm practices – information, feedback, consultation, and the active promotion of solidarity or support groups tend to lead to increased demand, greater adoption of new practices, and better utilization of services.

(Bhatnagar and Williams 1992b: 4, emphasis added)

As another staff member has put it, 'the benefits of a participatory approach is not simply the immediate advantage of a project better tailored to the client's needs, but the impulse it gives to the long term process of *changing mentalities*' (Landell-Mills 1992a).

The African crisis and the emergence of governance

The concepts of 'governance' and 'good governance' were first publicly introduced by the World Bank in a 1989 report, *Sub-Saharan Africa: From Crisis to Sustainable Growth*. The report argued that 'underlying the litany of Africa's development problems was a crisis of governance' (World Bank 1989: 60). This idea of a 'crisis of governance' went beyond simply a concern with failing government institutions and focused attention on a much broader set of political and social factors.

Ultimately, better governance requires political renewal. This means a concerted attack on corruption from the highest to the lowest levels. This can be done by setting a good example, by strengthening accountability, by encouraging public debate, and by nurturing a free press. It also means empowering women and the poor by fostering grassroots and non-governmental organizations, such as farmers associations, cooperatives and women's groups.

(World Bank 1989: 6)

The rise of a concern with the 'governance' of its borrower countries sees the final consolidation of the view that successful economic development is dependent on a radical programme of political, institutional and social transformation.

It was the development experience of sub-Saharan Africa that provided the initial impetus behind the emergence of a concern with good governance. The 1989 report was the fifth report on the development problems in sub-Saharan Africa published by the Bank during the 1980s, and no other region received such sustained critical attention (World Bank 1981, 1983b, 1984, 1986a, 1989). In 1984 a Special Office for African Affairs was established, and again this was unique to sub-Saharan Africa. In 1987 the Special Facility for Africa was set up to provide additional fast disbursing loans to the region, and this again was unique. More significantly, it was becoming clear, even on the Bank's own analysis, that Africa was experiencing a sustained economic crisis. Per capita food production was lower in 1989 than 1980, and only one quarter of the population of the region had experienced rising per capita food consumption during the same period. Export volumes had declined, external debt was rising, primary school enrolments had fallen during the decade, and investment rates had fallen by 25 per cent since 1980. On top of all this, sub-Saharan Africa was still experiencing rapid population growth (World Bank 1989: 17, 21, 22, 25). The Bank argued that taken together these generated a 'growing sense of helplessness' inside and outside the region (World Bank 1989: 23).

While sub-Saharan Africa had been experiencing dramatic economic decline during the 1980s, the Bank had doubled its lending to the region, up from an average of US$1,921.5 million per year (1980–1986), to US$3,932.9 million in 1990 (World Bank 1991b: 110). According to its own evaluations, however, less than 50 per cent of all Bank financed projects in the region were rated as 'satisfactory' in terms of development outcomes, the lowest of all regions. Sub-Saharan Africa had the worst record of any region in Bank financed agricultural sector projects, the worst success record in institutional development projects, and less than 20 per cent of adjustment related technical assistance projects were rated as 'substantially effective' again the worst record of any region (World Bank 1994b: 70, 117, 133; Jayarajah and Branson 1995: 245). This record was a serious challenge to the World Bank. It was becoming clear that World Bank activities were not having the development impact they were expected to produce, and in many instances seemed to have produced very few long-lasting benefits: 'traditional recipes are certainly not working as effectively as we expected. Whether it is structural adjustment or institutional development, somehow things are not jelling adequately' (Agarwala 1990: 51). Some staff were even beginning to argue that structural adjustment was unlikely to succeed at all in Africa, largely because African economies were characterized by inadequate infrastructure, low levels of education and institutional and capacity weaknesses (Elbadawi *et al.* 1992: 506).[5] A decision was taken within the Africa Technical Department that only a long term perspective on the problems and possibilities facing sub-Saharan Africa could offer any hope of 'light at the end of the tunnel', both for the Bank and the region. In addition it was thought that only such a report could overcome the threat of 'donor fatigue' which accompanied the growing sense of helplessness about the region (Agarwala and Schwartz 1994: 3).

A broad outline for such a report was presented to the Board of Directors in February 1987. It was at this stage that the idea of extensive consultation/participation by the wider development community and especially by Africans emerged, and was strongly supported by the Board and the Africa Vice President, Kim Jaycox. It was thought that this would help legitimate the report's conclusions in the eyes of the wider development community and in sub-Saharan Africa itself. The Bank was explicitly trying to generate a consensus around its agenda for African development; a consensus which had been noticeably lacking in debates over structural adjustment (Agarwala and Schwartz 1994: 4; Agarwala 1990: 52). The consultation/participation process in the preparation of the report consisted of four activities (Agarwala and Schwartz 1994: 6–9). First, Bank missions visited 14 African countries to discuss with government officials, academics, donor representatives, NGOs and representatives of the private sector a number of 'issue' papers prepared by Bank staff and 'African development professionals' (World Bank 1990a). Second, Bank missions visited donor countries and international organizations and held meetings with governments and academics. Third, drafts of the report were sent to a number of NGOs and discussed at a UN–NGO conference in Geneva. Finally, ideas in the report were discussed in a workshop on regional integration and cooperation held at the Arusha Conference in late 1988. In all, a total of 233 Africans and 109 non-Africans were 'participants' in this 'participatory process' (Agarwala and Schwartz 1994: 32). It remains unclear exactly what impact this process had on the report's content. The report certainly *looked* different from any of the others the Bank had produced about sub-Saharan Africa. It had an extensive bibliography (which the previous sub-Saharan Africa reports did not) and it was accompanied by four volumes of background papers, many of which were either implicitly or explicitly critical of the Bank's activities in the region. One of the co-authors of the report has said that the report's orientation was 'influenced in a fundamental way by the oral and written inputs of Africans and the development community [and that] one could even suggest that the participatory process brought about a veritable shift in perspectives, and in the paradigm underlying the report's analysis' (Agarwala and Schwartz 1994: 10). Another possibility is that this process reinforced already existing ideas within the Bank about the importance of governance issues in sub-Saharan Africa. Whatever the case, the report marked a significant step in the evolution of the Bank's thinking about sub-Saharan Africa and development in general.

First, the draft report signalled a recognition that the obstacles to development success in the region ran deeper than simply misguided economic policies and failing governmental institutions. Among these obstacles the draft report particularly identified political, social and cultural factors. It suggested that 'prices and markets could not deliver' without a solid institutional, social and cultural basis for governance and development management. It also argued that one of the key problems in sub-Saharan Africa was the existence of 'consumptive [*sic*] elites' and the associated problems of corruption and over-consumption. These attitudes and patterns of conduct were damaging the ability of African economies to save and invest, and hence develop productive industries. Second, there were criticisms of donors, including the Bank, for their inflexible and top-down stance to recipient governments, which it was argued should be replaced by a bottom-up, demand driven, and increasingly participatory approach which could generate 'borrower ownership' of development projects and programmes. Third, as part of an attempt to go beyond a purely 'economistic' approach to development, the draft report argued the necessity of considering indigenous values and institutions in the modernizing process. 'The consensus that emerged ... was that development can only succeed by building on one's strengths and it can only be sustained if it grows from one's historical/traditional roots', and there is an 'interaction between endogenous evolution and modernization'. Fourth, the draft report recognized the importance of the informal/non-formal sector (the 'missing middle'), and the importance of NGOs in a vibrant non-state sector. Fifth, the draft report recognized the significance of wider institutional issues such as the legal and regulatory framework in determining development success (Agarwala and Schwartz 1994: 16–24). One if its co-authors said that 'many of the conclusions in the draft report appeared to be at variance with the Bank's philosophy and practice' (Agarwala and Schwartz 1994: 28).

Because of this, consensus within the Bank over the arguments in the draft report was 'shaky at best', and the authors of the report were accused, among other things, of excessive romanticism about the informal sector and the role of African traditions, and of downplaying the centrality of economic growth in favour of a broader notion of social development (Agarwala and Schwartz 1994: 28–9). This reaction led to a new principal co-author, Stanley Please, being brought in to help rework the report into a form more acceptable within the Bank. The choice of Stanley Please was important for the subsequent acceptance of the report because he was one of the advocates of the Bank's move into structural adjustment lending in the early 1980s and had the reputation of being a firm advocate for neoclassical economics (Please 1984, 1990). The draft report was 'toned down' for publication: 'the unorthodox findings ... could only be presented in a low profile manner, more as an undertone than an open challenge' (Agarwala and Schwartz 1994: 27). Much that was significant in the draft report did survive this rewriting and editing. The published report said,

[i]t is not sufficient for African governments merely to consolidate the progress made in their adjustment programs. They need to go beyond the issues of public finance, monetary policy, prices and markets, to address fundamental questions relating to human capacities, institutions, governance, the environment, population growth and distribution, and technology.

(World Bank 1989: 1)

It argued that 'governments and donors alike must be prepared to change their thinking fundamentally in order to revive Africa's fortunes' as 'top-down approaches [to development] demotivated ordinary people' (World Bank 1989: 2, 3). It indicated that the Bank should rethink its attitude to the role of the state in development:

[t]he state has an indispensable role in creating a favourable economic environment ... It is of the utmost importance for the state to establish a predictable and honest administration of the regulatory framework to ensure law and order, and to foster a stable, objective and transparent judicial system.

(World Bank 1989: 55)

The report emphasized the importance of decentralization in the process of building better governance: 'local governments are best suited to meet the needs of local communities ... developing competent and responsive local governments is central to capacity building' (World Bank 1989: 58). The report also stressed the need to harness and encourage 'civil society'. It suggested that the 'new approach should try to reconcile efficient government with the common desire of individual Africans to be independent economic operators, and of social, religious, and community groups to play their part':

the object should be to release private energies and encourage initiative at every level. At the grassroots level this means village and ward associations; at the intermediary level, various local nongovernmental and cooperative unions and other organizations; at the national level, chambers of commerce and industry, trade associations umbrella NGO organizations ... and professional associations of Bankers, doctors, lawyers, accountants and the like.

(World Bank 1989: 59)

The report argued that these 'intermediaries' can voice local concerns, bring a broader spectrum of ideas and values to bear on policy making, and exert pressure on public officials for better performance and accountability (World Bank 1989: 61). Finally, the report stressed the need to recognize the importance of social and cultural conditions in African countries. 'To be successful, development programs need to take fuller account of a country's social context and cultural dynamics', and 'a sound strategy for development must take into account Africa's historical traditions and current realities. This implies above all a highly participatory approach' (World Bank 1989: 60).

The final report, and especially the concept of good governance, received a great deal of attention outside the Bank. Some commentators argued that the report and the idea of good governance was just another way for the Bank to 'blame the victims' and ignore its own role in perpetuating underdevelopment in Africa (George and Sabelli 1994: 142). Others suggested that the report replicated the argument of the Berg Report that Africa's crisis was caused by over-interventionist states, and accused the Bank of hypocrisy in demanding that African governments be accountable and transparent, while the Bank itself was not (Parfitt 1993). It was argued that the continued pursuit of structural adjustment which the report advocated was inconsistent with its emphasis on human development and 'putting people first' (Stein and Nafziger 1991). Some suggested the Bank was getting involved in arguments about the relationship between democratic government and economic growth, while others saw the report as trying to be too comprehensive and visionary, or as an attempt to consolidate the 'Bank's expert status' in the field of African development, and manufacture a consensus around the Bank's interpretation of the region's development problems (Emmerson 1991; Collier 1991; Gibbon 1993).

Whatever the particular merits of each of these responses they missed a significant aspect of the report. It presented a vision for the future of African countries which was that of a modern market economy supported by effective and efficient institutions, and a vibrant non-market sector or 'civil society'. The report makes it clear that the 'traditional recipes' including structural adjustment are not enough. The attempt to create a modern market economy must be much more all-embracing, recognizing the role that social, cultural and political factors play, and it must tackle those social, cultural and political formations which are obstacles to development. As Pierre Landell-Mills suggested, 'to be workable the governance of African states needs to be *systematically rebuilt from the bottom up*' (Landell-Mills 1992a, emphasis added).

4 Governance, liberalism and transformation

The specific ideas of governance and good governance took up only a relatively small part of the 1989 report, but it was this which caused the most controversy within the Bank (World Bank 1989). The internal debate over governance centred around three related questions. First, what exactly was meant by the term? Second, what could the Bank do to promote good governance while remaining within the restrictions imposed by its Articles of Agreement? Third, what should the Bank do given its knowledge and experience in this area? This debate was given added impetus by the fact that many major bilateral aid donors were reorientating their aid policies towards promoting democracy, human rights and 'good governance'. By the end of the 1990s, however, the idea of 'good governance' had become a central part of the World Bank's policy platform. This chapter traces the consolidation of good governance within the Bank. The last section of the chapter then links the discussion of liberal theory in chapter one to the policies of good governance.

Good governance beyond the World Bank

In 1990, the British Foreign Secretary said that 'countries which tend towards pluralism, public accountability, respect for the rule of law, human rights and market principles, should be encouraged' (Hurd 1990). In January 1992 the British Foreign Aid Minister said that components of 'good government' included getting rid of corruption, restricting military expenditure, encouraging transparency, political pluralism, regular free and fair elections, the rule of law, freedom of expression, respect for human rights and an independent and efficient judiciary (Chalker 1992). In 1991, USAID published a 'Democracy and Governance Policy Paper' which said USAID would support the strengthening of democratic representation, support the participation of citizens in the political process, support the promotion of human rights and lawful government, and encourage 'democratic values' (USAID 1991). Francois Mitterrand said in 1990 that France would link its aid contribution to efforts designed to lead to greater liberty and democracy (Mitterrand 1990). The German Ministry for Economic Cooperation said that in assessing its aid contributions it would use criteria which included political participation, responsible and accountable government and respect for human rights (Van de Sand and Mohs 1992). During the same period many other bilateral and multilateral donors committed themselves to promoting democracy, respect for human rights and 'good government' (Carothers 1994a, 1994b).

Good governance within the World Bank

In this atmosphere there was confusion within the Bank over the precise meaning of 'governance', and especially over whether 'good governance' was synonymous with democratic government (Serageldin 1990). This confusion was heightened by a few passages in the 1989 report which seemed to hint at such a link. The report said that 'history suggests ... political legitimacy and consensus are a precondition for sustainable development', and it noted that the two countries with the best economic performance in sub-Saharan Africa, Botswana and Mauritius, both had effective parliamentary democracies (World Bank 1989: 60, 61). The report nowhere actually advocated democracy or multiparty elections, but in an atmosphere in which other donors were advocating democracy, some Executive Directors and the World Bank's Legal Department were worried a concern with good governance was going beyond the remit of the Bank's Articles of Agreement. Article IV(10) states that '[t]he Bank and its officers shall not interfere in the political affairs of any member; nor shall they be influenced in their decisions by the political character of the member or members concerned', while Article III 5(b) states that the Bank shall make loans 'with due attention to considerations of economy and efficiency and without regard to political or other non-economic influences or considerations'. In a meeting at the World Bank Legal Department in late 1990, it was argued that given these restrictions, the only possible justification for the promotion of democratic institutions by the Bank was if it could be demonstrated that they were 'inherently linked to the process of economic development as a *means*', but it was also argued there was little convincing evidence for this (Serageldin 1990, emphasis in original). On the other hand, those governance issues which were linked to economic development (or 'economy and efficiency') as a means, could legitimately be taken into consideration by the Bank in its dealings with borrower countries.

This argument was at the heart of the World Bank's General Legal

Council's ruling on the extent of Bank activities in the realm of governance allowed by its Articles of Agreement. The ruling argued that 'economic considerations, in their broad sense, do extend to the manner in which the state manages its resources, and may thus become difficult to isolate from political considerations' (Shihata 1991a: 70–1). 'Political events' he argued, 'may have significant direct economic effects which ... may properly be taken into consideration in the Bank's decisions'. He argued that 'technical considerations of economic efficiency', rather than ideological and political preferences should guide the Bank's work at all times, and among these 'technical considerations', were included civil service reform, legal reform, accountability for public funds, and budget discipline. These were the components of governance with which the Bank could legitimately concern itself as they had significant direct economic effects. He argued that it was only by staying within these concerns that the Bank would maintain its status as a 'quintessential technocracy' (Shihata 1991a: 53, 75, 82, 83, 95).

At the same time, the Board of Directors was pushing the Bank's management to produce a more comprehensive report on the various dimensions of governance and its implications for Bank operations. Responsibility for producing this report was given to the Policy Research Department of the Bank. This was important because the resulting report would be a more general Bank policy report, which ensured that governance issues would be dealt with as a matter of concern for the Bank as a whole, not simply the Africa region. The drafting process was even more lengthy and disputed than the 1989 report. By one account it went through at least 17 drafts. Nonetheless, when it was presented to the board only two Executive Directors objected (China and Iran/Iraq/Saudi Arabia). The Board's acceptance of the report has much to do with the Shihata ruling, as well as the fact that by this time many bilateral donors were committing themselves to similar policies.

The report defined 'governance' as 'the manner in which power is exercised in the management of a country's economic and social resources for development'. 'Good governance', the report argued, was 'synonymous with sound development management', and it stayed within the Legal Council's ruling by identifying governance issues as those which relate directly to economic development (World Bank 1992b: 1). The report identified four areas of governance necessary for sound development management: improving public sector management, increasing governmental and administrative accountability, reforming legal systems, and improving information provision and transparency. Before detailing the content of the report it is important to examine its theoretical underpinnings because this had a major impact on its reception within the Bank. Although the 1989 report's recommendations on governance might have accorded with a 'common sense' understanding of African development problems based on direct experience, they were not anchored in any theoretical analysis of why governance issues were important for economic development. The 1989 report had not shown any cause/effect linkages between good governance and economic development either statistically or theoretically. This was a problem to the extent that it contributed to a scepticism which many within the Bank felt about the idea of good governance.

Running alongside the preparation of the 1992 *Governance and Development* report, was the preparation and publication of the 1991 *World Development Report*, subtitled 'The Challenge of Development' (World Bank 1991a). Chapter seven of that report, 'Rethinking the State', neatly encapsulates the Bank's understanding of the role of the state in development at the time. It affirmed that wherever possible economic activities should be the preserve of the private sector. It used a new political economy analysis of the role of interest groups, the emergence of 'predatory states', 'rent-seeking' and corruption, and it suggested a number of remedies including civil service reform, rationalizing public expenditure, privatizing state owned enterprises and expanding the role of NGOs (World Bank 1991a: 129–31). The report argued that the democratic nature of a government was not the most important consideration, and it pointed instead to the crucial role 'institutions' were thought to play in development.(World Bank 1991a: 133). Institutions were defined broadly to include 'the conventions that govern the way people deal with each other'. The report argued that institutions had been a 'major force' in economic development historically, by defining property rights, enforcing contracts, and establishing norms of behaviour adapted to the 'needs of a modern market economy' (World Bank 1991a: 134–5).

The team charged with producing the 1992 report on governance consciously drew on these arguments as they provided a theoretically grounded way of arguing for the importance of governance issues in economic development. The 1992 report argued that,

> with respect to rules, without the institutions and supportive framework of the state to create and enforce the rules, to establish law and order, and to ensure property rights, production and investment will be deterred and development hindered. This is because high 'transaction costs' will inhibit such activities.
>
> (World Bank 1992b: 6)

The report argued that institutions (broadly understood) determined the performance of economies by creating a structure of incentives that confronts economic agents and which may be more or less conducive to engaging in economically productive activity. These arguments were also applied to the internal operations of bureaucracies. In particular the report drew on the literature surrounding the 'principal-agent problem', which relates to how a 'principal' (the government or a senior bureaucrat) can most effectively and efficiently induce their 'agent' (a government agency or lower level bureaucrat) to act in the way the principal would wish (Eisenhardt 1989). This pointed attention to issues surrounding information provision within bureaucracies, monitoring mechanisms, and incentive structures that could ensure congruence between the wishes of the 'principal' and the actions of the 'agent'. It was argued that adequate flows of information within bureaucracies would reduce inefficiencies and so improve the delivery of essential services. This in turn was thought to require improved accountability and transparency within bureaucracies, and between bureaucracies and their 'clients'. In this way governance concerns could be theoretically anchored: a vibrant economy requires an efficient and effective state to create and enforce rules which reduce transaction costs for economic agents; and to get an efficient and effective state requires accountability, information provision and transparency. For internal Bank consumption this was a significant advance, as governance concerns could be shown to be theoretically important in an economistic language of transaction costs, exchanges and information, and this proved to be vitally important for the increased acceptance of these issues outside of the Africa Region of the Bank.

What the *Governance and Development* report said about the four issues it identified as lying within the Bank's Articles of Agreement is largely unsurprising. Improving public sector management was well established as an important issue for the Bank and included civil service reform and public expenditure management (World Bank 1992b: 12). The report argued that accountability was required inside bureaucracies and between service delivery agents and recipients. It identified two 'levels' of accountability. 'Macro-level' accountability required improved financial accountability through systematic auditing and accounting and increased accountability for the economic performance of parastatals and bureaucratic departments. Mechanisms for 'micro-level' accountability included the familiar ones of competition in service provision ('exit') and participation ('voice'). The report suggested that decentralization could be a link between these two levels by reducing the overloading of central government and improving access to decision making by groups in society, and all these are important ways of reducing corruption (World Bank 1992b: 15–28). The legal framework was important for creating a stable and predictable environment for economic actors and should include a set of rules known in advance, effective enforcement of those rules, and an independent judiciary (World Bank 1992b: 28–38). Improved information provision and transparency were important because they reduced transaction costs by reducing uncertainty and risk in economic activity. Information about market conditions and government policies help create an 'enabling environment' for the private sector, and within the government, information provision and transparency help ensure effective monitoring and reporting of activities and helps reduce corruption. Finally, it is important that there are information dissemination channels so that groups in society (including NGOs) can hold governments accountable (World Bank 1992b: 39–47).

The report also argued that Bank efforts to promote good governance should depend on the extent to which these efforts 'reflects the country's institutional needs, its history, its political economy, and the nature of its society', and that the 'current debate on governance ... needs to take account of cultural differences' (World Bank 1992b: 2, 8). There are difficulties with this position, to which we will return. Nonetheless, it indicated a genuine interest in 'culture' on the part of some Bank staff. First, there was a concern with the impact 'cultural traits' could have on the functioning of government agencies (Dia 1991, 1994). The 1989 report recognized that 'culture' can have an impact on the performance of bureaucracies, and argued that 'family and ethnic ties that strengthen communal actions have no place in central government agencies where staff must be selected on merit, and public and private monies must not be confused' (World Bank 1989: 60). Second, there was a concern with seeing how certain cultural traits or indigenous institutions might be integrated into the modernization process. The 1992 report cites the examples of Japan and other South-East Asian countries to support the view that development and the maintenance of 'cultural' traits are not incompatible (World Bank 1992b; Dia 1991).

The *Governance and Development* report was a major statement of the Bank's understanding of the components of governance and its role in promoting good governance in its borrower countries. Its use of New Institutional Economics as a theoretical anchor and the fact that it was not concerned solely with the development experience of Africa ensured that governance issues became a prominent area of concern in the Bank. Despite this, there was still a large amount of scepticism on the part of many Bank staff about just how important the issues of 'good governance' really were, and whether they could be adequately integrated in World Bank operations. Between 1992 and 1999, however, the concept of governance was to be increasingly integrated into Bank policies. The acceptance of governance was greatly helped by two developments. First, there was a debate within the Bank over its internal operations and its developmental effectiveness, and in this debate the ideas of good governance became associated with the perceived need to improve the Bank's development impact. Second, some of the issues associated with governance came to be seen as important in explaining the economic success of a number of South-East Asian countries. The increased acceptance of governance issues in explaining development success and failure continued through 1997, when the role of the state in development became the focus of a World Development Report and the Bank appointed a new Chief Economist, Joseph Stiglitz, who was committed to the idea that governance and institutional issues were important for the future success of Bank lending. Finally, by 1999, good governance on the part of the Bank's borrower countries was seen by the President of the Bank as a 'prerequisite' for sustainable development.

The Wapenhans Report

An extensive internal debate over the operations and effectiveness of the Bank was initiated by Lewis Preston who became World Bank President in 1991. In February 1992, Preston invited retiring Vice President Willi Wapenhans to head a 'Portfolio Management Task Force'. This task force was to review, among other things, the quality and scope of loan supervision, the project and programme design process, the Bank's internal review mechanisms, the internal processes for collating and disseminating lessons learned from projects and programmes, the handling of poorly performing projects, the quality and utility of project reviews, and the role and quality of staff training (Portfolio Management Task Force, 1992). The significant thing about the subsequent report was not what it said, much of which had been said before by external commentators, but that these same things were now being said and accepted officially by the Bank itself. The report (known as the Wapenhans Report) found that one third of Bank projects were 'having major problems', including 42 per cent of those in water supply and sanitation, and that in 39 per cent of borrower countries, 25 per cent or more projects were having serious problems (Portfolio Management Task Force 1992; see also World Bank 1995a: 45). The task force also found that the time required for project completion was on average two years longer than that estimated by the pre-project appraisal, that borrower compliance with legal covenants was 'startling low', and that the gap between estimated economic rates of return at pre-project appraisal and at completion had increased (Portfolio Management Task Force 1992).

The report argued that some of these problems stemmed from the internal 'culture' and operations of the Bank itself (Naim 1994). It highlighted the undue emphasis on loan approval and said Bank staff had a 'pervasive preoccupation with new lending' which reduced the quality of projects it financed and downgraded the role of project implementation and monitoring. The report also said there was too little emphasis placed on the identification and assessment of major risks to project performance, especially the capacity of implementing agencies, and that poorly performing projects received too little attention (Portfolio Management Task Force 1992). The report argued that the project-by-project approach to portfolio management was ineffective because it did not identify or address sectoral or country obstacles to project success. Finally, the report argued that there had been too little accountability within the Bank for actual development impact, and that the internal Bank review and learning processes were inadequate (Portfolio Management Task Force 1992). The report stressed that over 70 per cent of Bank projects and programmes remained successful, but it was nonetheless a highly critical report.

These debates over the World Bank's performance were important for the increased acceptance of governance issues within the Bank. The Wapenhans Report itself argued that the 'regulatory environment' was an important determinant of project success, and that 'the borrower's institutional, managerial, organizational, and technical capacity to implement projects, and its capacity to audit managerial decisions all have a strong impact on project outcomes' (Portfolio Management Task Force 1992). The report also noted the importance of 'ownership' and the need for an 'intimate understanding of the workings of local society'. It recommended among other things that the Bank recruit more staff experienced in public administration and institutional development and that the Bank foster participation by borrowers and beneficiaries in project preparation. As we have seen in the previous chapter, these arguments were supported during this period by OED (World Bank 1995a; Jayarajah and Branson 1995; see also Picciotto 1995). Although the Wapenhans Report was never published by the Bank, its contents were widely known, and it was a very damaging report for the Bank whose self-image was that of the leading development agency and a repository of expert knowledge (Weaver and Leiteritz, 2005: 373–5).

Governance, institutions and the state

The 1992 *Governance and Development* report had ended by saying that 'much uncharted territory' remains to be explored (World Bank 1992b: 57). After 1992, the issues of decentralization, legal reform, civil service reform, the role of 'culture' and information systems all received critical attention within the overall framework of governance (Silverman 1992; Ehdaie 1994; World Bank 1995d; Rowat *et al.* 1995; Lindauer and Nunberg 1994; Nunberg and Nellis 1995; Serageldin and Taboroff 1994). The biggest research effort by far centred on the role of institutions in economic development. Some of this concentrated on exploring the implications of New Institutional Economics at a theoretical level (Picciotto 1995; Klitgaard 1995). In 1994, Douglass North spoke in a series of seminars at the Bank, where he argued that politics and 'political markets' were the key to successful economic growth. 'We can never say', he argued, 'we'll just let markets work, as if markets grew up on their own' (North 1994). North had an important influence in persuading many Bank staff of the importance of governance and institutional issues. The impact of New Institutional Economics fed into the large amount of research being undertaken within the Bank on the role of institutions and the regulatory framework in the development experience of East Asia (Campos and Lien 1994; Esfahani 1994). Much of this work grew out of the *East Asian Miracle* report (World Bank 1993a). This report was the result of several years of Japanese criticism of what they saw as the Bank's unduly free-market approach to development embodied in structural adjustment lending (Wade 1996). In 1991 the Japanese Overseas Economic Cooperation Fund (OECF) issued a paper about the Bank's structural adjustment policies (OECF 1991). By this time Japan was the second biggest shareholder in the Bank and had the largest bilateral aid programme of any donor (in monetary terms). The paper argued that direct promotion of investment by governments, selective trade controls, selected protection of infant industries, the subsidization of credit and government ownership of certain industries may all have an important role to play in the development process. The evidence for this, so the paper argued, came from the dynamic economies of East Asia and Japan itself. In essence, the OECF were asking the Bank to learn from East Asia, and the Japanese Ministry of Finance pressed the Bank to undertake a special study of the region, which the Bank agreed to on the condition that the Japanese fund the study

The report has been the subject of extended debate. In particular it has been argued that the report downplays the role of state intervention in *explaining* East Asian economic success: 'like Narcissus, all the Bank was capable of doing in its report was seeing the image of its own "market friendly" policies in East Asia's fortunes' (Amsden 1994: 627). What is important here is that the report recognized how East Asia governments had created a 'secure institutional environment for private investment' and had 'reputable' bureaucracies. The report argued that these reputable bureaucracies were the result, first, of pay scales which were sufficiently high to attract and retain good economic managers, second, the effective institutionalization of rules and procedures for bureaucrats, and third, the insulation of bureaucracies from political intervention. In addition, the report suggested that many East Asian countries had created institutions to improve communications between the government and private sector (World Bank 1993a: 352–3). Regardless of whether the report was an accurate explanation of East Asian economic success, it confirmed to the Bank the importance of institutional issues in explaining economic performance, and increasingly helped to legitimate these issues within the Bank. Most importantly, it brought into sharp focus that good governance was not simply about the strength of governments, but their capacity to collect, manage and use economic information, and to manage their links with societal groups effectively.

There were still debates over governance and institutional issues within the Bank during this period. First, it was said that the implementation of governance issues required skills and country specific knowledge which the Bank did not possess. Second, a concern with governance issues was still regarded by some staff as analytically and empirically 'soft', and as not having produced any specific operational recommendations. Third and following from this, some in the Bank argued that the Bank's record on institutional development was poor, and was likely to remain so unless the state of its knowledge improved. Fourth, it was suggested that expanded work in these areas would actually increase recipient dependence on the Bank, and so discourage borrowers from initiating their own reforms and hence reduce the 'borrower ownership' of projects and programmes. Despite these doubts, governance issues became an increasingly accepted part of World Bank policy.

The 1997 *World Development Report* took as its central theme the role of the state in development. In the same year, the Bank appointed Joseph Stiglitz as Chief Economist. There is a sense in which the changes in Bank policy can be charted through its various Chief Economists, from Hollis Chenery, to Anne O. Krueger, and Stiglitz. What is clear is that Stiglitz represented the acceptance within the Bank of the idea that the state has a crucial role to play in development, and that the success of development depends on good governance. One of Stiglitz's main theoretical contributions to economic theory has been to show that under conditions of imperfect information, and hence imperfect markets, governments could undertake interventions which made everybody better off. As Stiglitz has argued, 'because information is never perfect and markets never complete, [this analysis] completely undermined the standard theoretical basis for relying on the market mechanism' (Stiglitz 1996: 156; see also Greenwald and Stiglitz 1986). This did not resolve the question of how to develop a state which could undertake these complementary interventions effectively, but it did mean there was always a critical catalytic role for the state in development (Stiglitz 1989).

In his address to the 1997 Annual World Bank Conference on Development Economics, Stiglitz outlined his understanding of the process of economic development and the role of the state. He said that a 'striking lesson' to have emerged from the experience of the East European countries was 'how difficult it is for markets to get established – there is a rich institutional infrastructure, much of which requires government action to establish and maintain', and 'it may take a strong government to establish a strong market' (Stiglitz 1997). For development to be successful, government must take responsibility for creating laws and legal institutions, establishing clearly defined property rights, ensuring effective competition, enforcing contracts, and regulating the financial sector. This will require improving the performance of governments through accountability, incentive mechanisms, the use of market surrogates, improving the composition and quality of government employees, and improving systems of hiring, training and promotion (Stiglitz 1997: 8–11). In conclusion, he argued that 'an essential part of the new development strategies involves the creation of institutions and the changing of cultures – the movement to a culture of change and science, where existing practices are questioned and alternatives constantly explored' (Stiglitz 1997: 18).

The greatly expanded vision of development which the acceptance of governance issues entails was made clear by Stiglitz in a 1998 lecture (Stiglitz 1998). First, he argued it was necessary to stimulate the private sector. While this required a stable macro-economic framework, and the development of physical infrastructure, it also required well-developed legal and regulatory systems. Second, he argued there was a need to reform the operations of governments. Third, there was a need to develop social and community groups, in order that they can both interact with governments 'effectively' so that their participation in project design and implementation can be elicited, thus increasing their 'commitment' and 'ownership'. 'Participation at the community level allows the project choice to reflect the needs and preferences within the community ... Equally important, local participation engenders commitments ... and participation in the project itself becomes part of the transformation process' (Stiglitz 1998: 26). Finally, Stiglitz argued that 'in the end, the transformation of society entails a transformation of the way *individuals* think and behave' (Stiglitz 1997: 27, emphasis in original).

The significance of governance issues for the World Bank was also signalled in 1999 by the Bank President James Wolfensohn (Wolfensohn 1999).[1] First, he argued that one of the prerequisites for development is 'good and clean government'. This requires increased governmental capacity, 'open' government, a transparent regulatory system and an absolute commitment to 'clean government'. Second, it is necessary to develop an 'effective legal and justice system' and a well organized and supervised financial system. Third, it is necessary to develop and include 'civil society in all its forms' in the process of development in order to engender participation and ownership.

Good governance and liberal theory

> Good governance is epitomized by predictable, open, and enlightened policymaking (that is a transparent process); a bureaucracy imbued with a professional ethos; an executive arm of government accountable for its actions; a strong civil society participating in public affairs; and all behaving under the rule of law.
>
> (World Bank 1994a)

By the middle of the 1990s the Bank had been led to contemplate a detailed transformation of the politics, institutions and societies of its borrower countries. This is a liberal project of transformation. First, the ends and arrangements the Bank is trying to achieve are recognizably liberal ones. Second, these are justified by typically liberal forms of arguments. Third, the barriers to the achievement of these ends and arrangements the Bank has identified are also typically liberal.

Liberal spheres

In chapter one we argued that liberal thought has tended to cluster around four spheres – the state, the economy, 'civil society' and the individual. The fact that good governance is conceived of exactly in terms of these spheres is the clearest indication of how indebted to liberal thought the ideas of good governance are. The Bank, too, almost exactly replicates the ambiguities and tensions within liberal thought about these spheres. The Bank's discourse lacks the intellectual self-awareness of much liberal theory, but as we also argued in chapter one, this gives an insight into how liberal ideas are utilized in political practice, and, of course, it shows just how dominant these liberal understandings of social transformation are within the World Bank.

Good governance is in very large part about the state. And, like much of liberal thought, the World Bank sees the state as having the central role in constructing and protecting the conditions under which the achievement of liberal ends is possible. But as with liberal thought so this central role is fraught with tensions and ambiguities. In particular good governance is about making the state both stronger and weaker. It must be strong enough to govern effectively and enforce the rules. This is the significance of the concern with improving the institutional, regulatory and legal frameworks for development. It must also be strong enough to resist the malign influence of certain social groups. On the other hand the state must be made weaker. It must learn to govern less, and it must be made accountable to certain social groups. The state must be insulated and accountable, uncaptured and responsive, autonomous but not oppressive. As we shall see in the next chapter this takes the World Bank down the road of designing intricate development interventions that attempt to mediate this tension. So, for example, the state is to be given much enhanced tax-raising powers, yet it is also subject to carefully controlled practices of publicity and accountability. The one area where good governance does not simply reflect the debates within liberal theory is the issue of the neutral state. To be sure, the Bank has a concern with withdrawing the state from areas of economic life (as with structural adjustment) but beyond this it seems clear that when faced with obviously non-liberal social arrangements (ethnicity) the state must be made robustly non-neutral. The state can, perhaps should, be neutral between groups who already exhibit liberal patterns of association, but it is clear that until then the state is charged with furthering the liberal project of social transformation.

A key part of this is the construction of the conditions under which a market economy can function effectively. The good governance agenda signals a realization that the construction of this kind of economy requires a great deal more than reform of economic policy. It requires the construction of an intricate institutional framework to govern and encourage market-based economic transactions. And, as we shall see in the next chapter, the construction of the economic sphere extends to the construction of the traits necessary for the market to function at all. In all this the World Bank replicates liberal theory. There is the tension between the idea of the economy as a natural order, requiring only the liberation of people from oppressive institutions and policies, and the economy as a constructed order, requiring instead careful government action to bring it into existence. We have, too, the concern with ensuring that the pursuit of private interests remains largely within the economic sphere and does not spill over into the public realm (hence anti-corruption); yet, at the same time, as noted above, the state must be responsive to some kinds of economic interests.

These ambiguities are seen also in the World Bank's ideas about civil society. Good governance seems to require the construction of the right kind of 'civil society' that can both hold the state accountable for its actions and pressure the state into undertaking actions conducive to economic development. And again we can see how this reflects liberal thought. We have on the one hand the idea of civil society as a political institution, charged with holding the state accountable and in so doing ensuring the state pursues the public interest. On the other hand we have the idea of civil society as a private associational sphere that enables people to pursue their particular private interests (as businesses, unions) through political means – with the obvious danger that these groups exercise too much influence on policy making. It is also possible to see how the imagined composition of civil society within the good governance agenda reflects ambiguities within liberal thought. The kinds of groups the World Bank refers too tend to be recognizable modern and based on non-affective ties. And as we shall see, in practice the World Bank has designed development projects that encourage the formation of these kinds of groups. Groups based on affective ties are not considered to be part of 'proper' civil society.

The construction of a civil society is also part of the process for reconstructing the attitudes and behaviour of individuals. The World Bank has come down pretty clearly on the side of the view that in large part peoples' attitudes and preferences are constructed through membership of society, rather than being endogenous to society: it is culture rather than nature that really shapes how people think and act. And, as we shall see in the next chapter, it has undertaken development interventions designed to rework the habits and attitudes of persons. In this respect the World Bank mirrors the older tradition of liberal thought which, despite its obsessive concern with nature and reason, very often demonstrated that people were heavily influenced by such things as custom, tradition and religion. And, as we argued in chapter one, this provides the resources for the project of transforming these habits and attitudes. In sum, it is clear that the kind of social world the World Bank wants to construct is a liberal one. As we have been at pains to argue, this does not mean it is free from ambiguities and tensions; quite the reverse. But the tensions and ambiguities that exist within the good governance agenda themselves reflect the deeper and more profound tensions and ambiguities within liberal thought itself.

Liberal justifications

At the most general level the achievement of good governance is presented as a way of ensuring development success. Ibrahim Shihata has argued that improved public sector management and an effective legal system are some of the 'basic requirements for a stable business environment, [and] indeed for a modern state' (Shihata 1991a: 85). Kim Jaycox has argued that 'institutional capacity' is 'critical' to 'the development effort and the chances of success' (Jaycox 1995). Good governance is seen by the Bank as 'central to creating and sustaining an environment which fosters strong and equitable development' (World Bank 1992b: 1). These claims have a 'rule utilitarian' underpinning. Rule utilitarianism is the view that the utilitarian criteria of judgement should be applied to the basic set of rules and institutions within which individual acts take place (Harsanyi 1982). Conceived in this way, the Bank's project is thought to be good for people because it thinks that market based arrangements provide the best 'rule structure' for the achievement of material well-being. This justification does not preclude these institutional arrangements from being beneficial for others, say, Western governments or multinational companies, but it does rely for its suasive power on the idea that these ends are desirable because they are desirable for those within the Bank's borrower countries. This justification is recognizably a liberal one. From the very beginning of liberal thought, appeals to various forms of utilitarian or welfare maximization criteria have been used to justify certain desirable institutional arrangements.

The World Bank has given a number of other justifications for the pursuit of its transformative project. The World Bank's General Legal Council has said that some of the Bank's work can be understood as promoting certain human rights, such as a right to education, a right to health, freedom from poverty and the rights of women (Shihata 1991b). The Vice President for Environmentally Sustainable Development suggested that participation by project beneficiaries can lead to the 'empowerment' of poorer groups (Serageldin 1995: 98). The Bank has argued that its legal reform efforts can make an important contribution to the development of an 'equitable and just society' (World Bank 1994a: 23). These are familiar liberal justifications about the importance of individual rights, the desirability of political participation and the desirability of certain forms of equality (Salkever 1977). It is particularly striking how these other justifications are also tied to utilitarian arguments. The Bank's General Legal Council has drawn an explicit connection between human rights and economic development: 'pervasive human rights violations may ... have broader implications related to the country's stability and prospective creditworthiness' (Shihata 1991b: 133). Ismail Serageldin has argued that 'action to improve the status of women will be enhanced by efforts to increase civil liberties', that increased civil liberties are positively correlated with women's access to education, and that increasing women's access to education is essential for development because it reduces child mortality rates, increases life expectancy, and allows women to participate more fully in the process of economic development (Serageldin 1995: 50–8, 59). In addition, as we have seen, the participation of project beneficiaries and stakeholders is thought by the Bank to improve the chances of project success.

Where the actions of persons are seen to accord with the Bank's understanding of desirable ends and arrangements these actions are appealed to in the justifications for them. The Bank has argued that market-based economic arrangements are desirable because they accord with the actions of economic agents who respond to price incentives (World Bank 1981: 55, 1989: 91–3). The Bank is willing to build on 'indigenous' institutions and practices when they can be shown to support its understanding of what is desirable for persons in developing countries. The Bank has argued that 'many African values and institutions can support' the development process. These include the communal culture, respect for nature, informal credit systems which successfully draw on customary values and patterns of social organization, and indigenous cultivation practices (World Bank 1989: 60). A Bank staff member has argued that it is possible to use 'formalism and ritual' to reinforce contractual bonds, that African 'cultural values and traditions' can be used to 'stimulate productivity as well as alleviate internal conflicts and labour problems', and that it should be possible to 'expand extended family solidarity to the wider context of the enterprise and administration in Africa' (Dia 1994: 190–1).

Where the actions of persons do not seem to support the Bank's understanding of what is desirable, however, the Bank is more than prepared to ignore this and argue that such an arrangement really is desirable, even if the persons concerned do not know it. So for example, the Bank argues that tribal and other affective ties are not conducive to the effective functioning of bureaucracies, and so should not be taken as a sign of what those agents really should desire: 'in some spheres ... there can be little compromise. Family and ethnic ties that strengthen communal actions have no place in central government agencies where staff must be selected on merit, and public and private monies must not be confused' (World Bank 1989: 60). The same is true of other 'indigenous' institutions and practices. One Bank staff member has argued that certain African 'cultural traits' are not conducive to development. These include placing a higher value on inter-personal relations than on personal achievements, emphasizing conspicuous consumption over productive investments, and valuing leisure and the ability to engage in rituals, ceremonies and social activities over labour: 'clearly, the six to eight decades of colonialism were simply not long enough for both individuals and governments to develop a new national entity that could transcend ethnicity and the traditional decision-making system' (Dia 1991: 11–12; Dia 1994: 176–9). As Pierre Landell-Mills has argued, 'the challenge is to build on the elements that are compatible with modernization and development, [and reject] those that are not' (Landell-Mills 1992a).

The World Bank replicates the powerful tendency in liberal thought to 'strip away' the actual lived lives and manifest choices of persons, and ground justificatory arguments in the 'real' nature of persons, their 'real' interests, some account of what persons would choose if they knew what was in their best interests or in some entirely hypothetical choice situation. 'The liberal strategy has been to search for *underlying* interests and beliefs shared in common which may be appealed to in the justification of ... institutional arrangements' (Waldron 1987: 145, emphasis added). It is clear why this must be. Neither liberal theory nor the World Bank can appeal solely to the actual lived lives and real choices of persons for their justificatory arguments because these people cannot be relied upon to choose or prefer liberal arrangements.

Liberal sociology

Finally, and following from this, the World Bank, like many liberal thinkers, has identified several barriers to the achievement of what it considers to be the right ends and arrangements. These include ignorance, the influence of mistaken ideas and doctrines, the influence of custom and tradition, prevailing opinions, and the operation of insidious interests. In this the World Bank reflects to a quite remarkable degree much of liberal political thought. Kim Jaycox has argued that in many African countries there are only a 'tiny minority ... who know what they're doing' and that 'in many countries they're not capable yet of putting together plans which will solve their problems' (Jaycox 1995). Here Africans are simply ignorant of certain arguments and practices and so could not be expected to accept them. Again, Kim Jaycox has argued that 'ethnicity has ... gotten [*sic*] in the way of professionalism in Africa' (Jaycox 1995). Similarly, Pierre Landell-Mills has said that 'African managers cannot easily set aside their loyalties to their community ... African managers cannot easily escape the heavy social obligations that take up a large proportion of their time' (Landell-Mills 1992b). Here, prevailing opinions and customary patterns of conduct have prevented people from pursuing the right ends and arrangements. The Bank also argues that agents have been duped into accepting wrong arguments; that is, for some reason, people actually believe wrongly. They believed for example that 'markets would fail', or that in a market economy, 'profit margins would be excessive' (World Bank 1989: 91). Finally, the Bank has identified the operation of powerful interests as a central barrier to the pursuit of what it understands as desirable ends and arrangements. As has been seen in previous chapters, the Bank has argued that the interests of politicians, bureaucrats and groups have prevented the adoption of 'rational' economic policies.

Within liberal thought the identification of the origins of people's habits and attitudes begins to provide the resources for the development of techniques of transformation. If people are malleable then their habits and attitudes can be remade. As we saw in chapter one, many liberal thinkers have advocated more or less sophisticated programmes for the transformation of persons. And, as we will see in the next chapter, the World Bank replicates this in much of its development activities.

Conclusion

A concern with the governance of its borrower countries has led the World Bank to contemplate an all-encompassing liberal project of social transformation that extends not just to countries' economies, but also to their political, institutional and social structures, and the thoughts and behaviour of individuals. The expanding scope of Bank policies detailed in this and the previous chapter can only be understood against the background of the international normative structure examined in chapter two. The World Bank was an institutional embodiment of the internationally sanctioned objective of the domestic provision of material well-being through the pursuit of economic development. This always had the potential to come into conflict with the norms and practices associated with state sovereignty. In the early years of the Bank's operations a compromise was struck whereby the Bank would assist governments in their pursuit of a domestic economic project. This compromise relied on a particular view of the state and of the state's relations with its society. As detailed in chapter three this compromise unravelled as the state came to be seen as a major obstacle to economic development, as politicians and bureaucrats came to be seen as having interests directly opposed to those of society, and as it became clear that some states were manifestly not providing for the material well-being of their societies. The widening scope of Bank policies, and its increasingly interventionist development strategies, were then legitimated by this changed view of the state.

If this provides the general international normative background for understanding the expanding scope of Bank policies, it does not explain the detail of that policy nor how it emerged within the Bank. The last two chapters have tried to trace the ways in which new policy concerns made themselves felt within the Bank. At the most general level there was a complex and changing interaction between internal and external processes. A persistent internal factor has been the process of Bank learning through an examination of its own lending. There have also been extended debates within the Bank over many of these new issues, and at times changes in personnel (Presidents, Chief Economists) and particularly influential individuals within the Bank have been important in stimulating and reinforcing the acceptance of new policy concerns. External factors have included criticism of the Bank by other agencies such as NGOs and the US Congress, the Bank's response to crises, such as the debt crisis and the enduring development problems of sub-Saharan Africa, and more general intellectual movements, such as the re-emergence of neoclassical economics in the early 1980s, the New Political Economy, and New Institutional Economics. At particular times and over particular issues these internal and external factors have interacted in different ways. There still remains the problem of how the World Bank goes about trying to implement this transformative project. There is the problem, in other words, of what all this looks like in practice.

5   Transformation in practice

This chapter examines World Bank lending to improve 'governance' in Ghana. The aims of this chapter are twofold. First, an examination of the projects and programmes implemented by the World Bank is the only way we can see what the Bank's project of transformation looks like in practice. When we look at this practice we find that the Bank is engaged in an extraordinarily detailed and intrusive attempt to change large areas of social, political and economic life. Second, if the analysis so far in this book is plausible, we can expect an examination of the Bank's lending to tell us important things about what liberalism as a project of social transformation looks like in practice. In chapter one we argued that liberal political thought clustered around four spheres – the state, the economy, civil society and the individual – and that within these spheres liberal thought exhibited a number of characteristic tensions and ambiguities that were ultimately to be understood as related to the idea of liberalism as a project of transformation. In chapter four we argued that these can be traced though the World Bank's thinking about good governance. In this chapter we see how these tensions and ambiguities are exhibited in the lending practices of the Bank. This not only lends credence to the view that what the World Bank is doing is engaging in a project of transformation, but it also helps refine the account of liberalism by illustrating the kinds of concrete, practical issues liberals worry about. For example, while liberal political thought has not paid very much attention to the connections between liberalism and government information collection systems, as a matter of practice, improving the capacity of the state to collect and use information about its society has been a key part of the World Bank's strategy to improve governance.

Ghana is used as a case for three reasons. The first is simply that the World Bank has had a long-standing and intimate involvement with Ghana. This means there is lots of material to draw on, and it also allows for a certain amount of comparison over time in terms of the kinds of projects and policies the Bank has been pursuing. Second, relations between the government of Ghana and the World Bank have, generally speaking, been pretty good, and this means the Bank has had an opportunity to push for improved governance over a long period of time. Third, Ghana has not been afflicted by political instability that might disrupt the Bank's good governance agenda. Obviously, though, the case of Ghana can only be illustrative for the larger arguments about the World Bank, good governance and liberalism. There is a trade-off here between examining the Bank's lending in detail and showing that what the Bank is doing is similar in other countries. One of the criticisms of the World Bank over many years has been that it has a 'one size fits all' mentality. To the extent this is true we would expect the World Bank's lending in other countries to demonstrate similar concerns to that of Ghana. In this chapter, however, we make no attempt to show this. Instead we take the view that it is only by examining Bank lending in detail that we can get a proper sense of how ambitious the Bank's attempts at social transformation really are. In addition, the projects examined in the chapter are only a very small selection of the several hundred projects the Bank has funded in Ghana. Again, the inevitably selective nature of the examination is made up for by the opportunity to explore in detail the kinds of changes the World Bank thinks necessary for governance to be improved. Finally, it is important to note that this chapter makes no attempt to assess the success or failure of the Bank's attempts at social transformation. The object here is to show what this attempt looks like in practice. The following chapter will take up the issues of whether and to what extent the Bank can be expected to succeed in this attempt.

The World Bank and governance in Ghana

Ghana's economic trajectory since its independence in 1957 has been understood by many as a paradigm case of what went wrong with economic development in Africa (Jeffries 1989; Toye 1991; Killick 1978; Leith and Lofchie 1993). Until the early 1970s, Ghana's economy experienced stable, if moderate economic growth, reasonably low inflation, and only moderate government deficits. In common with many African countries, and fuelled by a mixture of nationalism and socialism, successive governments in Ghana associated industrialization with economic development, in much the same way as early development economics. Whatever the merits of this as an economic development strategy in the Ghanaian case, it is clear that the particular way it was implemented was a major contributory factor in Ghana's economic decline, which was exacerbated markedly in the 1970s by rising oil prices and falling cocoa prices. Successive Ghanaian governments intervened heavily in the economy through trade and exchange rate controls, government ownership of economic enterprises, and the procurement, transportation, storage and marketing of cocoa. Not only was this intervention more or less uncoordinated and fiscally unsustainable, but it was also associated with an eventual reduction in cocoa exports, and hence the government's main source of foreign exchange earnings (Leith and Lofchie 1993: 236–40).

Despite the onset of sustained economic decline in the early 1970s, successive governments refused to undertake economic policy reforms (Jeffries 1989: 79–80). From 1975 Ghana experienced an extreme economic decline that reinforced, and was in turn reinforced by, escalating political corruption, collapsing infrastructure and increasing social disintegration (Jeffries 1989: 77–80). After a period of political turmoil, Flt Lt Jerry Rawlings seized power in a coup on 31 December 1981, seemingly with mass support, or at least with little resistance from a population which had suffered increasing economic hardship. The first 18 months of Rawlings' government was characterized by a populism built around revolutionary rhetoric, popular political and judicial organizations, and a firm commitment to rid Ghana of political and economic corruption (Rothchild 1985). The economy continued to decline, and after a failure to obtain financial support from other 'revolutionary' states, the Rawlings government turned to the IMF and the World Bank for financial support in 1982, and in April 1983 the Economic Recovery Plan was begun, initially with support from the IMF, then subsequently the World Bank. Since then both organizations, but especially the World Bank, have been closely involved in Ghana's development policies and programmes.

It has become common to divide the structural adjustment process in Ghana into two 'phases' (Leith and Lofchie 1993). First, a number of administratively fairly simple or 'stroke of the pen' reforms, which were designed to restore macroeconomic and fiscal stability, and second, a number of politically and administratively more difficult reforms which were designed to establish the conditions for sustained economic growth, and actually achieve a structural transformation of the Ghanaian economy. There is little doubt that the first phase of structural adjustment was a success (Toye 1991: 159–70). The economy was stabilized, inflation was brought down from 123 per cent in 1983 to 25 per cent in 1986, growth was restored, investment levels rose from 4 per cent of GNP in 1983 to over 10 per cent in 1987, export volumes increased, government finances were stabilized, tax collection rose and with balance of payments support from the IMF, the level of imports increased (Toye 1991: 165–7). After 1987 the World Bank increasingly took the lead in setting the economic reform agenda in Ghana. The structural adjustment programme began to incorporate a more wide-ranging set of concerns including reform and privatization of state-owned enterprises, civil service reform, improved public sector management, financial sector reform and increased investment in human development as well as programs to mitigate the social costs of adjustment. Despite continued economic growth, it was in a number of these areas that institutional weakness became apparent, forcing the Bank to turn more explicitly to institutional reform and capacity building issues (Toye 1991: 179–83; Leith and Lofchie: 273–9). These issues became even more important as Ghana made the transition to multiparty democracy. In the election years of 1992, 1996 and 2000, the macroeconomic policy environment deteriorated rapidly. In addition to this, in 1999 and 2000 Ghana experienced a severe terms-of-trade shock as prices for its gold and cocoa exports fell and the price of its petroleum imports rose. Since 2000, Ghana's macroeconomic situation has been more stable and growth rates have improved.

The World Bank has been concerned with Ghana's governance right from the early 1990s. In 1993 the Bank produced a Country Strategy Paper (CSP) for Ghana which argued that Ghana needed to create an 'enabling environment' for private sector growth by removing 'inhibiting regulations', increasing transparency and due process in the enforcement of rules and regulations, divesting state owned enterprises, correcting tax 'distortions', reducing transaction costs in the financial sector, and conforming to 'international conventions' in such matters as accounting, auditing and the disclosure of financial and operating data (World Bank 1995b: 33–4, 1992c). It also argued that there needed to be improvements in public sector management, which included continuing the civil service reform program, improving expenditure management, improving tax collection, and 'capacity building' at both the central and local government level (World Bank 1992c: 91–5, 1995b: 34). An OED report on World Bank activities in Ghana (1995–1997) argued that 'improved governance is essential'. Included in this, so the report argued, was further progress on decentralization, improvements in the regulatory and legal environment, civil service reform, and improved accountability, particularly concerning the government budget (World Bank 2000b). The World Bank's 2004 Country Assistance Strategy for Ghana included many of the same concerns. It argued that improvements were needed in coordination between ministries; that the capacity of local government institutions needed to be improved; that the civil service needed to be 'professionalized'; that the government's financial management needed to be strengthened; that corruption needed to be reduced; and that participation by civil society in the management of public affairs needed to be encouraged though increased provision of information on government business (World Bank 2004b). The World Bank's on-going support for Ghana's Poverty Reduction strategy illustrates the same themes. Nominally the government of Ghana was responsible for producing its Poverty Reduction Strategy. In fact, as Lindsay Whitfield has argued, the World Bank was the most important influence on the content of the report (Whitfield 2005; see also Fraser 2005). Unsurprisingly, then, the strategy involves the creation of a governance framework characterized by a democratic, inclusive and decentralized state, a capable and motivated public service, and an effective policy, budget management and implementation process. The World Bank has argued that Ghana needs to do much more to achieve this objective. Again it has stressed the importance of improving the capability of local government, reform of civil service, strengthening the capacity of the central state, improving the budget management process, improving accountability and transparency, and reducing corruption (World Bank 2003a).

Two points are worth noting from this brief review. First, the World Bank's governance concerns have been fairly consistent over time. Again and again it has stressed the importance of civil service reform, improved budgeting, improved coordination among ministries, decentralization, improved accountability, and regulatory and legal reforms. Second, this is an ambitious and far-reaching agenda. There is almost no aspect of Ghana's political, economic and social life that the World Bank has not in one way or another concerned itself with. It is hard to know what, exactly, the sovereignty of Ghana means under these conditions, especially considering that the Poverty Reduction Strategy, supposed to be produced and thus 'owned' by the government, is in fact the result of substantial World Bank influence, and exactly reflect the kinds of policy priorities the World Bank has been advocating for the best part of a decade.

The state

Reform of the role and operations of the state is at the centre of the World Bank's attempt to improve the governance of Ghana. Here we examine World Bank lending under three headings: redefining the role of the state, improving coordination and capacity within the state and decentralization.

Redefining the state

Redefining the role of the state has been at the heart of World Bank thinking on development from the early 1980s when structural adjustment became an important component of its lending. A concern with good governance, however, has involved more than just attempts to reduce the size of the government through privatization and civil service reform programmes, it has also involved a systematic attempt to redefine the relationship between the state and 'civil society' and the 'private sector'.

In 1996 the Bank undertook a Public Enterprise and Privatization Technical Assistance Project (PEPP) in Ghana which was designed to help the government implement its public enterprise reform and privatization programme (World Bank 1996a). The privatization of State-Owned Enterprises (SOEs) has been part of the economic recovery programme since 1983, and it continues to be a key part of the Bank's strategy, as is the reform of those SOEs which will remain under government control. In 1994 the public sector accounted for an estimated 35 per cent of GDP, including 40 per cent of manufacturing activity, and almost all the financial sector and utilities. As of 1994, about two hundred enterprises remained in public ownership which employed approximately 150,000 employees. SOE liabilities to the government exceeded US$1 billion at the end of 1994, and the government had guaranteed approximately US$250 million of SOE borrowing. The reform and privatization of SOEs was one area in which Ghana had not complied with Bank loans conditionalities, and while there were political and ideological factors behind the governments unwillingness to engage in a process of mass privatization, there were also technical and administrative problems associated with a lack of expertise in valuing the assets of SOEs, a lack of information, a lack of clarity in the legal code, and lack of bureaucratic coordination (Leith and Lofchie 1993: 276–9; Toye 1991: 180–1).

One particular problem identified by the World Bank was that the State Enterprises Commission (SEC) had no accurate information on the value of these enterprises, and no accurate information on the exact fiscal burden they were placing on the state (World Bank 1996a: 4). One component of the PEPP supported the Ministry of Finance and SEC in developing a 'portfolio management capability' to allow the government to 'coordinate and manage the reduction of the size of the portfolio through divestiture, focus on core financial performance criteria, and address the new financial policy issues created by the privatization program'. In particular, it focused on maintaining complete and reliable information, monitoring and tracking the financial and operational performance of SOEs, and advising the government on financial policy issues (World Bank 1996a: 5–6). PEPP also provided funds to help reform the legal and regulatory framework for SOEs. This went beyond a change in the legal status of SOEs into limited liability companies, and encompassed measures to reduce government interference in the day-to-day management of SOEs, increase their exposure to 'market competition', and use 'incentives' to improve their performance and increase their accountability (World Bank 1996a: 7–8). In addition, the project supported the government in developing and implementing a 'public information and communications strategy', which would increase accountability by providing for public dissemination of information on the performance of SOEs, and which would build and sustain public and stakeholder support and investor confidence in the privatization programme (World Bank 1996a: 10).

The Bank's attempt to redefine the role of the state can also be seen in another project that has as one of its objectives the privatization and/or commercialization of nearly 200 government-owned or controlled agencies, ranging from the Ghana University Press and the National Theatre to the Ghana Tourist Board (World Bank 1999c: 73–7). The stated aims of the project are: 'redefining the role and function of the state, designing appropriate institutions and systems to implement this role, and rationalizing the existing structure and systems to meet the new design' (World Bank 1999c: 3). Part of this project is a fairly straightforward attempt to close down those agencies that have no clear mandate, and the project provides for severance pay and retraining. Those agencies that do have a viable mandate are to be reformed, and as far as possible either fully privatized or at least commercialized. It is expected that this will result in a reduction in staff, and again the project pays for severance and retraining. The overall aim of these components is to reduce government spending. But on top of reducing the size of the state, this project also attempts to reconfigure the relationship between the state and the 'private sector'. The aim here is the 'introduction of performance-based management principles for more efficient public services, with increased customer orientation, transparency and accountability' (World Bank 1999c: 8). Concretely what this means is increased private sector input into government operation through exchange programmes and joint activities, and increased private sector involvement in policy design and decision making (World Bank 1999c: 7). The idea is that this will not only make the government more efficient, but it will also increase accountability and transparency.

This concern with holding the state accountable to society is particularly clear in a recent Public Financial Management Project (World Bank 2000c: 3–4). This is a wide-ranging project focused on improving the budget management and revenue collection processes. But it also has as one of its key objectives the strengthening of monitoring and evaluation capacity, and the enhancement of 'stakeholder participation' and 'civil society' involvement in the area of economic management. This involves a number of components. First, it provides for reform of procurement procedures and the establishment of a new procurement oversight institution. Second, the project provides for capacity building for parliament to improve its oversight role in the area of economic management (this will help to 'professionalize its interaction with the government'). Third, the project supports capacity building for oversight agencies such as the Serious Fraud Office and for organizations within the Ghana Anti-Corruption Coalition (a 'civil society' organization) (see also World Bank 2000a). Fourth, the project funds a variety of initiatives to encourage the participation of civil society in the oversight of economic management. This includes providing training for the media so it can 'play its watchdog role' vis-à-vis the fiscal and economic activities of the government. Finally, the project funds reform of the information and public disclosure policies of the government.

Coordination, capacity and information collection

The Public Financial Management Project (PFMP) was one of a number of projects financed by the Bank which attempted to improve the financial and economic management capacity of the government of Ghana (World Bank 1996b). A long-standing theme of World Bank assessments of the state in Ghana has been problems with the coordination and management of public finances. The development of an integrated financial management system is seen by the Bank as critical to maintaining effective macroeconomic management and ensuring 'higher levels of accountability' (World Bank 1996b: 1, 2–4, 3–5). The PFMP was designed to improve the capacity of central government by creating an integrated financial management system to cover budget preparation and implementation, government accounting, cash management, aid and debt management, revenue management, procurement, and auditing. In each of these areas the project supported the development of systems which plan, process and report upon the government's financial resources. The management system is to be computer based, and the 'principal factor which "integrates" the system is a common, reliable, unified database to, and from which, all financial data flows, and which is shared by all financial users' (World Bank 1996b: 1–2).

The aim of the PFMP was to develop and institute a 'Medium-Term Expenditure Framework', which includes preparing expenditure profiles of all ministries and formulating a budget calendar. In addition, it supported the design of systems, processes and procedures for expenditure controls, such as checking for prior budget appropriations and verification for receipt of goods and services. The project also supported the implementation of a computerized system which could produce budget plans and monitor expenditures, as well as the training of a 'core group of budget and finance staff' (World Bank 1996b: 4–5). The PFMP sought 'to implant a modern accounting sub-system which classifies, records, and analyses in a timely, reliable, and standard manner all government financial transactions'. This included the formulation of a comprehensive chart of accounts which would link with the government's development plan and the national accounts, the introduction of a common ledger system throughout the government, and the specification of new accounting standards for the government which requires the introduction of new regulations for government-wide accounting. The development of a new accounting system would 'provide a window to the public to ascertain the financial status of the government [and would] serve as a major instrument in the formulation and implementation of government policies' (World Bank 1996b: 6).

The PFMP also supported the government's ongoing attempts to increase the efficiency of tax revenue collection, reporting, and forecasting, and the development of tax administration systems which are aimed at achieving greater taxpayer compliance. According to the Bank, the revenue collection system had a number of weaknesses, most particularly the 'lack of a unique tax identification number which would permit greater inter-agency collaboration and enable higher revenue collection'. The project supported the development and introduction of a unique and common 'Tax Identification Number' for each taxpayer, the development of a computer based tax system, and the enhancement of the tax audit and examination capacity of the Internal Revenue Service (World Bank 1996b: 8–9). It also supported the development of computer and monitoring systems for the collection of customs and excise duties, the development of a new 'Value Added Tax', as well as the education of taxpayers in tax payment and record keeping (World Bank 1996b: 9–10). Finally, this project provided funds for a number of initiatives to disseminate information on the status of the reforms to the donors and the private sector, including a 'Public Financial Management Reform Program Newsletter' which would be distributed within the government to donors and to the private sector (World Bank 1996b: 15–16).

In 2003 the World Bank funded a 'Land Administration Project' (World Bank 2003c). Although the focus of this project was different, the general concerns with improving the capacity of the central state and improving information collection are the same. The government of Ghana has been revising its land policy since the late 1990s. The aim of this has been to stimulate economic development through improving security of land tenure, simplifying the process for accessing land, developing the land market and fostering prudent land management. The Land Administration Project was designed to support these objectives. It has a number of components. First, it supports the revision of laws and regulation regarding land ownership and administration. This is seen as particularly important because there are a variety of different types of land tenure systems in Ghana, some tribal, clan or family based, some commercial, and some held by the state (Kasanga and Kotey 2001). This review will involve drafting new laws where appropriate and resolving conflict and overlap between different systems. One outcome of this component is expected to be the development of a more efficient land market as it would enable more secure and transferable land titles. It would 'instill order and discipline to curb the incidence of land encroachment, unapproved development schemes, illegal land sales, and land racketeering' (World Bank 2003c: 6).

A second component involves improving land titling, registration and information systems. The problem here is that – except in some urban areas – there is no adequate mapping or land registration system. This leads to boundary disputes, protracted litigation and the freezing of land that could be used for development purposes. It also leads to informal land sales and thus lost revenues for the government (World Bank 2003c: 7). The project supports the development of a land information system that would record the physical location of land parcels, the nature of its tenure, the rights held over it and the holders of these rights. This will involve photo-mapping process, the funding of land registration offices, the improvement of the Land Title Registry system, and improvement to the land development and building permit system. The project also supports the establishment of a 'National Land Valuation Database' with a view to improving the ability of the government to collect tax revenue.

Decentralization

The Ghanaian Government has undertaken a large programme of governmental and administrative decentralization (Crook 1994; Oquaye 1995). There are currently 110 District Assemblies (DAs) in Ghana, with each having 86 specific responsibilities, including various aspects of health service provision, the maintenance of buildings, roads and streets, provision of education, water and sanitation provision, and community development. The intention of the decentralization programme was that the DAs would have complete, devolved responsibility for policy formulation and planning in the sectors assigned to them, as well as for the management of investment projects and ongoing operations and maintenance activities within their jurisdictions. In 1992 the Bank undertook a study of the local government sector and found a number of problems and difficulties facing DAs (World Bank 1993c). First, the relationship between the DAs and central and regional government remained confused. Second, there was no effective fiscal decentralization and the DAs remained dependent on the central government for investment finance. Third, the DAs did not have the financial resources to undertake effective operations and maintenance of local infrastructure, leading to the deterioration of local services. Finally, many DAs did not have the technical capacity or trained personnel to plan and implement investment projects. In another study published in 2006, the Bank found much the same set of problems (Darlan and Anani 2006).

In addition, however, this study found that a key problem was conflict between Traditional Authorities and the District Assemblies. These Traditional Authorities are long-standing and very important parts of particularly rural Ghanaian life, and the study argued that they are a genuine platform for 'community empowerment and mobilization', but that they 'lack the necessary technical and managerial skills or experience to effectively address the growing challenges in the lives of their people' (Darlan and Anani 2006: 18; Rathbone 2000).

The Local Government Development Project (LGDP) was a US$55.5 million project designed to support the decentralization programme by providing for the rehabilitation of urban infrastructure and services, and the 'institutional strengthening' of DAs, through technical assistance and improved revenue raising (World Bank 1994d). One objective of the LGDP was to promote the sustainability and expansion of urban services by strengthening the DA's financial, technical and managerial capacities, supporting the government's decentralization program and 'promoting accountability and efficiency in the provision of infrastructure and services' (World Bank 1994d: 9). The institutional development component of the loan provides support for increased district revenue collection. The Bank sees increasing local revenue collection as essential if DAs are able to perform their operations and maintenance activities. The LGDP provides support for drawing up Revenue Improvement Action Plans (RIAP) for each DA, and a key component of these plans is to be an improvement in the collection of property tax. The most important constraint on property tax mobilization to date has been the lack of accurate and up-to-date information The project provides support for the establishment of accurate urban maps using aerial photography, and for the formalization of street names and addresses to allow an accurate role of rateable properties to be drawn up.[1] Once this has been done, the project provides support for new computer hardware and software for the Land Valuation Board to enable the automated production of rate demands, and improved billing and collection operations. In addition, training will be given to DA staff to 'enable them to maximize the revenue potential that will be available from the updated, comprehensive tax base resulting from the revaluation of rateable properties' (World Bank 1994d: 90–102). The information gained through the mapping of urban areas and the formalization of street names and addresses is an important part of improving the availability of information for urban planning and infrastructure development (World Bank 1994d: 97).

A second component of the project was an extensive programme of staff training and institutional restructuring. Training programs for DA staff were provided in financial management, accounting and bookkeeping, project planning, project management, and personnel management. In addition, training courses were run for DA Councillors and Members of Parliament on the functions of DAs and the role of DA Councillors (World Bank 1994d: 110–11). The institutional restructuring involves support for the formulation and implementation of 'institutional reorganization plans' aimed at reducing the number of DA departments and establishing effective internal structures, support for the establishment of effective policy and legislative oversight of DA operations, support for the establishment of 'District Management Teams', and support for a 'labor market approach to public employment' at the district level through the increased use of private sector contracting (World Bank 1994d: 105–7). Finally, the project supported the strengthening of central government's capacity to assist and monitor the activities of the DAs. This includes provision of training courses on the distribution of revenue sources between central and local government, training of Land Valuation Board Staff in the use of the new computers and the maintenance of property valuation lists, technical assistance to the Town and Country Planning Department in record-keeping systems, and support for changes in the legal and regulatory relationship between central and local government (World Bank 1994d: 87–8, 91, 95, 108, 111).

A more recent project tackled the problem noted above of the relationship between Traditional Authorities and DAs. One of the main objectives of the Promoting Partnerships with Traditional Authorities Project was to 'help focus the contributions/influence of Traditional Authorities in socio-economic development' (World Bank 2003d). The idea behind the project is to see if the Traditional Authorities in Ghana can be encouraged to play a larger role in the provision of health and education provision in rural areas. As the project document put it, 'the government is seeking ways to ensure sustainable changes in the state's role in development, and this would be an opportunity to look to place greater reliance on resourceful civil society organizations such as the Traditional Authorities' (World Bank 2003d: 3). The project supports a host of activities. These include: education for Traditional Authorities so that they can play a more significant role in improving the health status of the communities, and especially in reducing the incidence of HIV/AIDS infections; the mobilization of local communities under the leadership of the traditional authorities to provide financial and labour resources to rehabilitate primary schools; enhancing the capacity of the Traditional Authorities to engage effectively with local District Assemblies; and providing funds to identify needs for revision, codification and dissemination of traditional laws, and increasing the effectiveness of traditional law courts. It also provides for capacity building for these traditional authorities in the form of training in financial management and informational management.

Liberalism, the state, and social transformation

It is clear from these projects that the Bank is concerned intimately with the actual practices of government and the capacities needed to pursue them. One of the virtues of the work of Michel Foucault and others who have followed a similar line of analysis has been to render these mechanisms and techniques of government as an object of analysis. Foucault has called the constellation of governance capacities the Bank is attempting to create a form of 'governmentality' which is formed by 'the institutions, procedures, analyses and reflections, the calculations and tactics that allow the exercise of [a] very specific albeit complex form of power, which has as its target population' (Foucault 2001b: 219–20). The notion of governmentality was less concerned with the exercise of sovereignty over a physical territory, and more with the increased government of the 'social': 'in contrast to sovereignty, government has as its purpose not the act of government itself, but the welfare of the population, the improvement of its condition, and increase of its wealth, longevity, health, etc.' (Foucault 2001b: 216–7). This shift signals a change in the understanding of what a government or state is for. It no longer becomes simply about the maintenance of territorial integrity, or of internal order; rather, in this new vision of government, the actions of the government are directed at controlling and improving the lives of its populace. Foucault also argued that accompanying this shift was a dramatic increase in the monitoring and surveillance capacities of states, 'the development of power techniques oriented towards individuals and intended to rule them in a continuous and permanent way' (Foucault 2001a: 300). Foucault calls this kind of power 'pastoral power', by which he means the state's ability to know both its society as a totality, and each individual member of it, and its role in ensuring, sustaining, and improving the lives of 'each and every one' (Foucault 2001a: 307).

Associated with this change, and indeed implied by it, is a dramatic increase in the ability of government to 'discipline' its populace, and to generate the possibility for 'action at a distance' (Rose 1996).

> Discipline was never more important ... than at the moment when it became important to manage a population; the managing of a population not only concerns the collective mass of phenomena, it also implies the management of population in its depths and details ... [it] renders all the more acute ... the necessity for the development of discipline.
>
> (Foucault 2001b: 219)

The 'disciplinary gaze' of the state must be dramatically enhanced if it is to manage and act on its population in its 'depths and details'. As these projects show, the Bank considers this an essential attribute of any modern government, and is manifested in its concern with individual tax identifications numbers, accurate property registers, the formalization of addresses and the ability of the Ghanaian state to plan, manage and coordinate development activities. It is also manifested in the Bank's concern to generate the possibility of 'action at a distance' through the use of tax systems and tax identification numbers which generate increased 'self-compliance'. It should also be noted how building state capacity also means that the 'disciplinary gaze' of the state is turned upon itself, or, as Foucault has put it, it entails a 'disciplinarization of the state' (quoted in Gordon 1991: 27). The demands of planning, monitoring and coordinating government action require that the activities of the state, in its own depths and details, are also made available for view, for only in this way can the state learn, plan and act effectively. As Karl Polyani has noted, Bentham's panoptic principle of 'inspectability' had its applications not only for prisons and convicts, but also to ministries and civil servants (Polanyi 1957: 110).

Following from this, it is easy to see why Barry Hindess has argued that liberalism is a project of government. In this view Liberalism is an *ethos* and *techne* of government. The *ethos* of liberal government is not to govern too much so as to disrupt the freedoms necessary for the market economy to function; the *techne* is to develop mechanisms which allow the state to govern and manage its population 'at a distance' without resorting to coercion which would undermine economic freedom, and destroy the legitimacy of the state. The Bank's lending to improve governance offers some support for this view. But while it is true that liberalism is intimately concerned with governing, the attempt to create effective forms of liberal governance is about creating the ability to pursue a project of social transformation. The concern with establishing a land valuation database, for example, is not simply to govern, but to change social relations by developing a land market and formalizing land tenure. Similarly, the desire to increase the accountability of the state is not simply to encourage it to govern better, but to encourage certain forms of associational life and certain kinds of social relations at the expense of others.

The economy

The World Bank has got well beyond the stage of thinking that simply 'liberating' the economy from undue state intervention and regulation will lead to sustained economic development. They do think that reducing intervention is important, but they have also recognized that much more extensive interventions are necessary. The two projects examined here – one dealing with financial institutions and the other targeting small enterprises – illustrate this well as they involve extensive institutional engineering as well as extensive 'education' components designed to equip people with the skills and attitudes necessary to thrive in the market economy. These projects show the extent to which the economy has to be constructed.

The Bank has argued that Ghana's financial system is not very 'deep', meaning that compared to other developing countries, even in Africa, Ghanaians keep much more money in cash and invest in building materials, or inventories, rather than saving in bank accounts, especially deposit accounts (World Bank 1995e). The Bank has attributed this low confidence in the financial sector to high levels of inflation, low or negative interest rates, high transaction costs and violations in the confidentiality of bank accounts in the early years of Rawlings' government (World Bank 1995e: 43; Aryeetey 1994). The problem, according to the Bank, was that this led to low levels of investment which hampered growth, and it led to low levels of credit availability which hampered the ability of the government to privatize state owned enterprises successfully. In addition, the cheque clearance and settlement system was slow, there was inadequate availability of information, and a lack of technological infrastructure needed for money markets and the nascent Ghanaian stock exchange to develop further (World Bank 1995e: 3–8). Finally, the overwhelming dominance of cash in the economy was constraining the government's ability to improve tax collection because when most economic payments are in cash it is difficult for the government to estimate incomes and revenues and monitor completed transactions (World Bank 1995e: 42).

The Bank hoped to expand and deepen the financial sector in Ghana by undertaking an institutional development project targeted at certain 'non-bank' financial institutions such as the Ghanaian Stock Exchange, the Securities Regulatory Commission, the Bank of Ghana, and institutions associated with the national insurance and social security system. The Non-Bank Financial Institutions Assistance Project aimed to 'strengthen institutions and introduce instruments which would create conditions to encourage substantial amounts of savings held in informal, non-financial assets to move to the formal financial sector where they can be used more productively'. In particular it aimed to create new legislative and regulatory frameworks, change organizational structures, increase operational efficiency, build capacity in each sub-sector, and promote institutions to improve the provision of financial services to the informal and rural sector. This was expected to 'create an environment conducive to greater private sector activity' as well as supporting the divestiture of state owned enterprises (World Bank 1995e: 11). Among the components the project financed include those to support the purchase of computers for the Ghana Stock Exchange to speed and monitor the payment and settlement process, as well as support for an educational campaign 'to increase the awareness and understanding by the local population of the role of the securities market in the context of the divestiture of public enterprises and the development of the private sector'. The project supported improving the capacity of the Social Security and National Insurance Trust, and assisting it to develop benefit schemes for workers in the informal sector most of whom do not contribute social security or national insurance payments. The project funded a review of the legal and regulatory role of the Securities Regulatory Commission and an increase in the capacity of the Bank of Ghana to regulate other financial institutions. It also included a specific component to improve the cheque payment and settlement system by changing the legal and regulatory environment surrounding cheque payment, upgrading the data communications system and increasing the number of automated teller machines. Finally, the project provided funds for a review of the institutions and mechanisms which provide finance for small rural and informal enterprises, and funds a pilot project to assess the feasibility of using small financial institutions – based on models such as the Grameen Bank in Bangladesh – in the Ghanaian context (World Bank 1995e: 16–32).

In a later project the Bank tackled the issue of micro and small enterprises (World Bank 2005e). The rationale for this project is revealing. The project document noted that despite GDP growth rates in the 4 to 5 per cent range over much of the previous twenty years, the structure of the Ghanaian economy has remained broadly the same as it was at independence. One reason for this, so the Bank argues, is that there remain significant barriers to the further development of micro and small enterprises. These include regulatory barriers, limited access to credit and finance, low skill levels and a lack of 'entrepreneurial appetite' (World Bank 2005e: 2, 34–8). The project funds a number of components that are designed to enable small enterprises to develop in such a way as to expand employment opportunities, boost GDP, and reduce poverty. First, the project funds an extensive programme of training and capacity building for Ghanaian banks so that they are better able to respond to the particular needs of small and medium enterprises. Also included in this is a partial credit guarantee scheme whereby a scheme is established to cover 50 per cent of net principle default loss of new loans provided by local banks to small enterprises.

A second component of the project covers capacity building and 'entrepreneurship development' for small enterprises. Part of this will be a programme of technical assistance in skills such as how to apply for loans, preparing financial statements, drawing up business plans, and education in strategic planning and business management (World Bank 2005e: 7–8, 51–62). The other part of this is a programme to 'promote entrepreneurship development through projects aimed at enhancing economic opportunities and promoting demonstration effects through various incubation processes' (World Bank 2005e: 11). What this means in practice is that the project will fund a series of small 'business parks' in textiles, furniture and information technology, whereby 'entrepreneurs' will have access to facilities and information that will, so the project suggests, encourage them to set up or expand their own businesses. A third component of the project funds changes in the legal and regulatory environment including speeding up the business registration process and reforming the process of standardization, certification and accreditation.

The first point to note about these projects, as with others we have looked at in this chapter, is how extraordinarily detailed they are. This indicates not only the institutional complexity necessary for economic development to be sustained and the 'governmental' capacity to achieve, coordinate and monitor this, but also the importance of institutions which are designed to draw people into the formal economy. Both of these projects are designed to create institutions which will be able to 'reach out' to individuals and groups which currently are not part of the formal market economy. This institutional reform is designed to incorporate people into the formal economy so that their savings can be tapped for increased credit provision and their productivity can be enhanced. In so doing these projects are also designed to give the government more control over its economy by making increased amounts of economic activity amenable to government action, particularly control of the economy through monetary policy, and so provide increased means for producing 'action at a distance'. In addition, the education and 'capacity building' components of these loans are designed to persuade people of the desirability of these institutional arrangements, and to inculcate certain habits, attitudes and patterns of behaviour. That is, far from taking for granted the existence of a utility maximizing individual who will automatically respond to changing incentive structures, these projects are actually attempting to persuade persons to enter the formal economy, and to equip them with the skills for doing to. These projects illustrate the *techne* of liberal government which involves the creation of institutional arrangements which allow the government to act to change behaviour without resorting to coercion or force, by bringing individuals into the purview of the mechanisms of government through their incorporation into the formal economy. Finally, these projects illustrate how central an agency the state is in the construction of a functioning market economy, and how robustly non-neutral the liberal state actually is within the liberal project.

Civil society

It is clear from the general discussion of the World Bank's understanding of good governance, as well as the detail of some of the projects discussed above, that it sees 'civil society' as having an important role to play in holding the government (central and local) accountable. The then World Bank country director in Ghana said in 2000 that the two main benefits of greater civil society involvement were the generation of feedback to help the public sector improve its performance and the improved accountability of government (Harrold 2000). In addition to this there has been a marked increase in the use of NGOs in project implementation and service delivery in Ghana (in line with the generally increased level of cooperation between NGOs and the World Bank) (Gary 1996). What is less obvious, but what is revealed through some of the World Bank's lending is the extent to which the World Bank is actively engaged in building a 'civil society'. Three projects that involved 'community development' make this clear.

The Community Water and Sanitation Project (CWSP) was a US$27 million project designed to support and implement the water and sanitation sectoral investment plan in Ghana (World Bank 1994e). The project was designed as a full-scale demonstration of Ghana's National Community Water and Sanitation Strategy which emphasized the provision of water and sanitation services to communities who are willing to contribute towards the capital costs and the operations and maintenance costs of water and sanitation facilities. This approach was in deliberate contrast to previous Bank water supply projects which have been of a 'top-down' nature with little community participation. As a result, water supply facilities had been installed with little consideration for demand and sustainability, and 'communities often saw no clear relationship between services rendered and tariffs charged'. Involving communities in decision making, and making them pay some of the costs of water supply facilities was seen as a way of ensuring the 'ownership' and sustainability of investments in water supply (World Bank 1994e: 1, 7–8, 28–31). District Assemblies, NGOs and partner agencies disseminated information about CWSP, and helped interested communities prepare an application for a construction grant. Communities had to demonstrate that they could effectively operate, maintain and repair water facilities, collect revenue, keep records and accounts, and evaluate and resolve problems (World Bank 1994e: 7, 38, 81). Once it had been established that the community could meet the requirements for involvement, a contract was drawn up between the community and the partner agency, or NGO. At this time the community was required to show proof that cash contributions from its members had been deposited in a specially created bank account. Communities were expected to contribute 5 to 10 per cent of the capital costs of the project and then levy and collect tariffs to pay for operations and maintenance (World Bank 1994e: 22, 28, 39).

All communities which participated in the programme were also required to participate in hygiene education and training programmes to 'encourage behaviour and conditions which help to prevent water and sanitation-related diseases'. It was envisaged that the project would 'break with the didactic, lecture-based approach which treats villagers as passive objects for one-way information transfer and is largely ineffective for bringing about behavioural change'. Instead, the project 'would adopt the participatory techniques of modern adult education, which are much more effective in inducing behavioural change'. Women in particularly were targeted, and the hygiene education messages would be 'reinforced' and 'legitimated' through radio broadcasts. In addition, there would be a programme of hygiene education in selected schools, which would also receive money to improve their latrines. This education component was expected not only to improve hygiene in schools, but because 'children are a highly effective means of introducing messages to adult households, and are particularly sensitive to peer pressure, they may thus become an important element in persuading their parents to construct latrines, or to support a water supply project' (World Bank 1994e: 85–6, 90).

A second Community Water and Sanitation Project ran from 2000 to 2004 (World Bank 2005d). Much the same themes were in evidence. Again the project targeted community capacity building and community hygiene practices. Again community groups were given training in planning, implementing, operating and maintaining water and sanitation facilities. More emphasis was placed in this project on the participation of women in community water and sanitation groups. The idea of combining community capacity building with other development objectives was again visible in the Community Based Rural Development Project (World Bank 2004d). In this case the project supported the development of rural infrastructure and the rehabilitation of community facilities, alongside capacity building community based organizations. Building the capacity of these organizations will, so the project document suggested, improve good governance and lead to the empowerment of the poor by encouraging them to participate actively in issues which affect their daily lives (World Bank 2004d: 4–5). Concretely this means they will be provided with 'capacity building' to enable them to 'identity and prioritize their needs', plan development programmes, access funds and manage and maintain local facilities. This means training in management, small enterprise development, 'groups dynamics', planning, budgeting, record-keeping and managing back accounts. In addition, small contractors and 'local entrepreneurs' will be trained in the basic skills for organizing labour intensive construction projects (World Bank 2004d: 36).

The Bank has also been attempting to change the behaviour, attitudes, habits, and mores of individuals and groups through its lending for the education sector (World Bank 2004a). Despite extensive reform efforts, up to two-thirds of the population remain, in the Bank's phrase, 'functionally illiterate', and of those who have received formal education, 40 per cent have lapsed into illiteracy due to a lack of appropriate reading materials. On the basis of survey data the Bank estimated that in the country as a whole only 35 per cent of the population could read, only 32 per cent could write and only 48 per cent could do simple mathematics. In addition, the rates of functional literacy were much lower in rural areas, and were consistently lower for women in both urban and rural areas. The Bank has estimated that no age group achieved a literacy rate of more than 50 per cent (World Bank 1992d). The Literacy and Functional Skills Project (LFSP) was a US$31 million project designed to support the Ghanaian Government's functional literacy program. The project's objectives were to expand the existing literacy programme to allow 840,000 adults to participate, to ensure that all 'new literates' have access to an expanded range of reading materials in Ghanaian languages, to expand the coverage of the FM broadcasting system, and to increase the frequency of educational broadcasting in the Ghanaian languages (World Bank 1992d: i).

The project was expected to have a number of benefits. Increased literacy is a 'means to economic, social, and political development, and [is] a first step towards the introduction of a more systematic approach to problem solving'. It can help 'give people the necessary consciousness, attitudes, skills and knowledge so that their creativity can be applied to further national development' (World Bank 1992d: 1).

> Through provision of basic literacy and numeracy skills, and new knowledge and attitudes, the program has the potential to have a positive impact in all areas of development (family planning, health, agricultural productivity, environmental protection, and the discouragement of negative and dangerous social customs). The program is also intended to regenerate popular involvement in community development activities.
>
> (World Bank 1992d: 10)

'Without a literate peasantry it is unlikely that significant increases in agricultural yields … will be possible', and 'any sustainable democratic system based on grass roots participation is only possible with a literate population'. After participating in the program, adult learners will be 'better prepared to address some of the issues central to their lives', including 'protecting themselves in commercial transactions' (World Bank 1992d: 26–7).

As a result of World Bank appraisals, several changes in the literacy programme were recommended. First, teaching should move away from 'syllable drills' towards a modified 'Freireian' approach based on key words and slogans. Second, more emphasis should be placed on 'functional messages' and incorporating community development activities into class teaching. Third, the teaching of functional numeracy should be stressed to allow learners to 'calculate in the market and in other areas of financial transaction'. Fourth, the programme should address the 'special needs' of women. A new set of lesson topics for adult learners was drawn up which included family planning, teenage pregnancy, community empowerment, killer diseases (particularly AIDS), income generating activities, traditional and modern farm methods, management practices, fish farming, the marketing of fish, soap making, poultry keeping, energy saving devices, child labour, intestacy law, drug abuse and communal labour (World Bank 1992d: 14, 35). To help motivate learners, they will each receive a set of materials free of charge, including an exercise book, a slate and a pencil. In addition, 'to help learners see the connection between what they learn and the self-improvement and development activities, each literacy participant will be provided with a few small development inputs' which would be directly related to the lesson topics. Finally, as a way of introducing some competition among learning groups within a district, 'and also of forging links between literacy and income generation', the top two literacy groups in each district will be allowed to access a credit facility to support small-scale income generating activities. The groups would have to prepare proposals and would receive training on setting up and running a bank account and repaying the loans (World Bank 1992d: 16–17).

These projects are designed to promote community groups and instill in individuals an understanding of the functioning of a market economy, and the skills, attitudes and patterns of thought and conduct which the Bank thinks necessary if the market economy is to flourish. It is clear from these projects that the Bank wants to encourage the development of particular kinds of groups in this 'engineering' of civil society (Williams and Young 1994: 98–9). These are groups which can see a 'clear relationship between services rendered and tariffs charged', who can keep records and accounts, who can 'demonstrate the capacity to manage and implement' projects, and who have the understanding and capacity to repay official loans. That is, these groups are to be composed of individuals who have the skills necessary to function in the institutionally complex market economy, and who are to be encouraged to engagement with the formal structures of the state and the economy. These kinds of groups seem to be what the World Bank has in mind when it advocates the promotion and development of a 'civil society'. This is not to be composed of groups bound by affective ties, but rather recognizably modern associations, bound by their common interests in engaging with the market economy, and who are thus brought within the purview of the state. These projects are also designed to induce behavioural change, to make people see the connection between 'services rendered and tariffs charges', to develop the skills necessary to manage a bank account, undertake 'promotional activities', keep accounts, discourage 'negative and dangerous social customs', develop a 'more systematic approach to problem solving', and 'calculate in the market'.

The individual

Within the projects examined above there have been a large number of components designed to change the attitudes, habits and mores of individuals; and developing the 'governmental' capacity of the state is bound up with the ability to influence the conduct of individuals in society. It is clear, for example, that the use of Tax Identification Numbers for all taxpayers is designed to increase the rate of self-compliance with the tax code, as is the development of accurate information about rateable properties, the formalization of addresses and the establishment of accurate information about land ownership. One thing these are designed to do is to help the government regulate the conduct of individuals in society by making individuals aware of the tax codes, and of the government's direct presence in their lives. The techniques used by the Bank to make these changes do not involve compulsion, or simple argument, but rather they work on the individual, trying to manage the process of individual choice and action to ensure consent (Williams 1996). They work, in other words, on the will of persons, but this is always mediated through something else, through the provision of incentives, through children, through education, 'capacity building' or 'traditional authorities'. Just as the individual is at the heart of liberal thought, so the individual is at the heart of the World Bank's attempt to construct 'good governance'. But rather than being simply liberated from oppressive institutions and practices, individuals are subjected to ever more intrusive disciplinary techniques designed to construct the 'right' kinds of skills, attitudes and habits, and to construct certain kinds of social relations. As with liberalism more generally, so the project of good governance has at its heart the transformation of the way people think and act.

Conclusion

The projects examined in this chapter demonstrate the extent to which the World Bank is engaged in detailed and intrusive development interventions. The Bank has concerned itself with government capacity, institutional restructuring, and the transformation of groups and individuals in a very detailed way, down to the syllabus of literacy programs, the education of community groups in marketing and accounting, the training of staff in financial institutions, and the management and collection of information. They also show that many governance issues, from participation, NGO cooperation, institutional reform, decentralization, accountability, public sector management and legal and regulatory reform have all become integrated into the Bank's lending. The governance vision is comprehensive, and for all the talk of building on 'indigenous' values and institutions, universal. It is of a 'governmental' state, able to monitor and direct its society, an institutional structure which will support and expand a market economy, and a society made up of groups and individuals who have attitudes, habits and mores suited to the market economy and liberal social relations.

These projects also reveal the extent to which the tensions and ambiguities in liberal thought are expressed in the Bank's lending. The state must be made both stronger and more accountable (to the right groups). The economy must be constructed in detailed ways, and economic conduct must be made visible to the state (taxation for example) and subject to regulation. Civil society must be engineered through encouraging the right kinds of social groups who can hold the state accountable for its actions. And, we noted above, individuals, for whom ultimately all this development activity is supposed to be good, will bear the brunt of the creation of new forms of discipline and new forms of governmental power.

6 Sovereignty, development and the liberal project

This chapter turns to some of the broader implications of the World Bank's pursuit of 'good governance'. First, it asks what state sovereignty can mean under the conditions detailed in the previous chapters. Second, it asks whether the kind of project of social transformation the World Bank is engaged in is likely to be successful or not. Third, it turns to the normative question raised in the introduction. Finally, it makes some concluding comments about the connections between liberalism and international relations.

Sovereignty and the liberal project

It is hopefully clear from the forgoing chapters that the World Bank's project of social transformation is ambitious and detailed. It involves almost all aspects of social, economic and political life, and it involves quite remarkably intricate interventions in the minutia of Ghanaian social, political and economic life. It is worth asking what sovereignty means for a country like Ghana where outside agencies are designing education programmes and establishing accounting standards for local communities. This erosion of sovereignty is all the more clear when one considers that there are a very large number of other development agencies at work in Ghana and in Africa more generally. Carol Lancaster has estimated that there are about 40 major bilateral and multilateral aid agencies active in the region (five of which disbursed over US$1 billion in 1996). In addition to this there are many smaller governmental and non-governmental organizations providing aid (Lancaster 1999: 38). For example, it has been estimated that there are something like 180 of these organizations at work in Burkina Faso (Carlsson *et al.* 1997: 44).

All these donors have embraced the idea of good governance. USAID is committed to strengthening the rule of law and respect for human rights, promoting democracy, encouraging the development of civil society, and promoting more transparent and accountable governance (USAID 2005). The Japanese Ministry of Foreign Affairs has argued that 'good governance is an essential foundation for the implementation of effective aid' (Government of Japan 1999). UNDP has argued that 'the ability of developing countries to fulfil their development goals is dependent upon the quality of governance' (UNDP 1998). The British FCO has argued that the promotion of human rights, democracy and good governance are essential components of sustainable development (Foreign and Commonwealth Office 2005). In November 2000 the EU Council of Ministers and the European Commission incorporated the promotion of human rights, democracy, the rule of law and good governance as an integral part of development co-operation (European Commission 2001). One could go on.

This is illustrative of an understudied but very significant shift whereby development agencies, both bilateral and multilateral, as well as many development NGOs, have become more integrated into a single 'development community'.[1] Dissenting voices among significant development institutions have almost vanished. Many of the various aid agencies are linked together through formal and informal arrangements. NGOs, for example, are often used as implementing agencies by larger aid organizations. The various organizations at work in any one country often engage in (more or less successful) coordination of their development activities. There is a pattern of rotation of staff from one agency to another (De Walle 1997: 65). Many of these organizations have relationships of various kinds with academics, researchers, 'development consultants' and government officials. It is this that leads James Morton to call the 'aid machine' a 'bureaucratic-academic complex' (Morton 1996: 56). The World Bank retains a dominant place among these others agencies (Stern and Ferreira 1997). 'In a policy world obsessed with the belief that only "global expertise" is valuable, the Bank has no real rival. The regional development banks and UN agencies fall over themselves to cooperate with the Bank, anxious to get a piece of the action from the large loans that may follow' (Goldman 2000). According to Robert Wade the Bank's dominant position is sustained by the sheer size of its lending, by a research budget that far exceeds all other development agencies and by its ability to attract global media coverage of its major research findings (Wade 1996).

What this means concretely is, first, that lots of other donors are pursuing projects with the same ambitious scope and the same level of detail, and second, that at the level of development strategy, recipient countries are increasingly facing aid donors as a unified bloc. Under these conditions it is not clear that 'sovereignty' means very much for states like Ghana (Williams

2003). There is very little commitment to sovereignty as a political value on the part of Western states and development agencies. The commitment to sovereignty has been trumped by a commitment to a liberal project of social transformation driven by the belief that the World Bank and other donors know what is 'best' for these countries. Within the normative structure of international politics, the tensions that existed between sovereignty and liberal ends and arrangements have been 'resolved' in favour of the pursuit of liberalism.

There are a number of possible responses to this. One is to say that states have never been completely sovereign and that there has always been external intervention in the internal affairs of states (Krasner 1999). This is true. But this kind of argument should not obscure the fact that what is happening in countries like Ghana is not just intervention in the internal affairs of states, it is a wholesale disregard for the idea that there is a realm of internal affairs over which the government should be considered sovereign, and over which external agents, as a matter of principle and a matter of practice, should not have any authority. Sovereignty has lost its significance as an institution that structures relations between states like Ghana and outside agencies. In this sense the World Bank's pursuit of good governance parallels the general downgrading of sovereignty associated with ideas such as 'sovereignty as responsibility' (Deng *et al.* 1996; International Commission on Intervention and State Sovereignty 2001). It is clear that sovereignty is no longer a guiding or constitutive norm in contemporary international politics, at least for a significant number of states.

The question this raises for the study of international politics is how, then, we should characterize these kinds of 'non-sovereign' relations; what is structuring relations between countries like Ghana and Western states and development agencies, if it is not a general commitment to the idea of sovereignty? It may be too early to give general answers, but one possibility is suggested by Mark Duffield who has argued that the 'securitization' of development has led to a fusing of the development agenda with the global governance agenda (Duffield 2001a, 2001b, 2002). As a recent USAID paper has put it:

> When development and governance fail in a country, the consequences engulf entire regions and leap across the world. Terrorism, political violence, civil wars, organized crime, drug trafficking, infectious diseases, environmental crises, refugee flows and mass migrations cascade across the borders of weak states more destructively then ever before.
>
> (USAID 2003)

Or, as James Wolfensohn put it, 'how do we better manage the big global issues – poverty, inequity, the environment, trade, illegal drugs, migration, diseases, and yes, terrorism?' (Wolfensohn 2004) Especially since September 11, the problems of 'weak' states have become seen as the most pressing issue facing Western states. The 2002 National Security Strategy says that 'the United States today is threatened less by conquering states than we are by weak and failing ones' (White House 2002). Condoleezza Rice has argued that states which are incapable of exercising 'responsible sovereignty' have a significant spillover effect in the form of terrorism, weapons proliferation and other dangers (Rice 2005). In an especially revealing phrase, the US Pentagon is seeking to develop a strategy to deal with what it calls the world's 'ungoverned areas' (the 'borderlands' indeed) (Patrick 2006: 4). The 'securitization' of development exposes developing countries to the desire on the part of Western states to govern those processes and issues that are considering potentially threatening. The fusing of development and security suggests that the pursuit of good governance is becoming increasingly bound up with the pursuit of global governance, and that the liberal project of social transformation being pursued by Western aid agencies is being increasingly understood in terms of building stable and 'friendly' states.

Development and the liberal project

A second response to the erosion of sovereignty is to say that it simply doesn't matter; sovereignty should be trumped by a commitment to 'development'. This is the logic of the idea of sovereignty as responsibility: sovereignty itself has no particular value, and it is only to be respected to the extent that states provide for the protection and material well-being of their citizens. The trouble with this position is that there are reasons to doubt that 'development' does indeed result from these interventions.

First, there are a set of problems associated with the kinds of relations that have been established between governments and donors such as the World Bank in countries like Ghana. The large number of external agencies at work and the extent and depth of their intervention have worked to undermine some of the objectives that donors want to achieve. Ghana, like many countries in sub-Saharan Africa remains heavily reliant on foreign assistance. For example, roughly 90 per cent of public investment expenditure is financed by aid flows, and during the 1990s aid flows amounted to about 10 per cent of GNP. Aid dependence can undermine a government's domestic legitimacy (if aid is seen by the populace as a symbol of external control) and thus erode the capacity of governments to enact and implement policy effectively (Lancaster 1999: 64). A World Bank paper has argued that aid dependence can undermine 'good governance' 'by weakening political accountability, encouraging rent seeking and corruption, fomenting conflict over control of aid resources, and alleviating pressures to reform inefficient policies and institutions' (Knack 2000). Many African governments, and many ministries within governments, have become more and more orientated towards satisfying external donors. This leads to a fragmentation of the overall development priorities for ministries, and often means that many African civil servants spend more time talking to donors than to other civil servants (Aryeetey and Cox 1997: 105).

The PRSP process has not substantially altered this situation. In theory the PRSP process is supposed to lead to greater country 'ownership' of development programmes by encouraging 'participation' in the process of defining development objectives and designing development strategies. In reality, the content of the poverty reduction strategies that emerge from this process have been almost identical with the development strategy advocated by the World Bank, and in addition, there are good reasons to be sceptical about the extent and impact of 'participation' within this process (Whitfield 2005; Fraser 2005). Rather than seeing the PRSP process as a way of overcoming the problems of accountability and legitimacy associated with extensive external intervention in Ghana's political, social, and economic life, they might be better seen as a way of increasingly legitimating this intervention.

Beyond the impact of the kinds of relationships established between governments and donors, there is the question of how successful World Bank lending has actually been. Assessing the effectiveness of development projects and programmes is notoriously difficult. First, there is the vexed issue of what 'effectiveness' might actually be. Should this be understood in narrow terms as an assessment of whether a project or programme achieved its stated objectives in the short-term? Or should it be understood in terms of longer-term sustainable impact? Or, alternatively, should it be understood in terms of its impact on broader development objectives (economic growth, poverty reduction)? Second, there is the obvious but deeply problematic issue of counterfactuals. The difficulty is 'controlling' the numerous factors that can influence development outcomes so as to assess the specific 'impact' of the particular project or programme. Clearly there are a host of exogenous factors (changing terms of trade for example) that can have a profound impact on the success or failure of development interventions. Third, and related, there is the issue of fungibility. The difficulty here is in assessing the opportunity cost of aid resources. This cuts both ways: in the absence of a particular aid project or programme what resources would have been spent, on what, and with what effects, by the government and other development agencies; in the presence of a particular aid project or programme, what resources are freed up to be spent by the government, on what, and again with what effects (Lancaster 1999)?

One route out of these problems has been to engage in large scale statistical studies (Cassen 1986: 35–41). This has been much favoured by the World Bank for example (World Bank 1998b). Despite the seemingly objective quality of the conclusions drawn from these studies, they are as open to criticism as any other kind of statistical studies of social phenomena. In particular there are problems with the quality of the data available, the extent to which the data is comparable (given different definitions and measures used by different countries), as well as the more technical problems associated with trying to capture complex interrelations using statistical techniques. Despite the efforts that have gone into these kinds of studies, the results have been disappointing. As Lancaster has put it, 'most of the econometric studies of the relationship of aid to growth have found that aid has had no significant impact, either positive or negative on economic performance' (Lancaster 1999: 44).

This may not be surprising given how causally complex the process of development actually is (Kenny and Williams 2001). But, of course, the fact of complexity is often forgotten by development agencies like the World Bank who want to claim that their particular policy concerns, such as 'good governance', are vital for development. Indeed, the evidence which would convincingly show that good governance really matters for development success simply does not exist. To be more precise, exactly what 'good governance' matters for is not at all clearly defined. For example, there is little evidence connecting improved governance with macroeconomic stability – another generally agreed upon precondition for development (Kaufmann 2004). There is also little systematic evidence linking improved governance with economic growth (Kenny and Williams 2001). As Arthur Goldsmith has argued, 'it is hard to say in advance that any particular institutional arrangement will bump up economic development' (Goldsmith 2005). Indeed, it is only recently that the World Bank has been undertaking a research programme into how and why good governance matters for development outcomes (Kaufmann *et al.* 2005a, 2005b). The best that we can say is that good governance might matter for development. But the ideas of good governance do not really reflect any particularly well-grounded account of how and why it matters; rather, of course, they reflect a commitment to the concepts, categories and arguments of liberalism, and a commitment to the idea that the World Bank really does know what is best.

Macro-level studies of the overall impact of aid on development don't tell us very much about the impact of individual projects and programmes. Some of the projects we examined in the previous chapter have run their course and the World Bank's own assessments of their success and failure is available.

As we can see the Bank's record is mixed. This is in line with the figures for project success and failure in Ghana and in Africa more generally. By the World Bank's own assessment, support for capacity building in Ghana over the last 10 years was only 'marginally satisfactory' (World Bank 2005c). In the period 1995–99 only 50 per cent of World Bank projects achieved even 'modest' institutional development impact (World Bank 2000b). The World Bank admits that it does not have a 'body of knowledge on what tools should be applied in different country and sector circumstances' to improve the success of capacity building projects in Africa (World Bank 2005b: xv). From 1995 to 1999 only 57 per cent of all World Bank financed projects in Africa were rated as 'satisfactory' in terms of development outcomes, and in only one-quarter of World Bank projects was the institutional development impact rated as substantial. For the period 2000–04 there had been some improvement in these figures, but still only just over half of World Bank projects were deemed to be sustainable and only 40 per cent had a substantial

Table 6.1 World Bank Assessments of Selected Projects in Ghana

	Outcome	Sustain- ability	ID impact	Bank performance	Borrower Performance
Public enterprise and privatization technical assistance project	U	L	M	U	U
Public sector manage-ment reform project	U	U	M	U	U
Public financial manage-ment technical assistance project	U	L	S	U	U
Local government development project	S	L	M	U	S
Non-bank financial institutions assistance project	S	L	S	S	S
Second community water and sanitation project	HS	L	S	S	S

Outcome: U = unsatisfactory, S = satisfactory, HS = highly satisfactory. Sustainability: L = likely, U = unlikely. ID impact: M = modest, S = substantial. Bank performance: U = unsatisfactory, S = satisfactory. Borrower performance: U = unsatisfactory, S = satisfactory.

Sources: World Bank 2002b, 2003d, 2004d, 2004e, 2005d, 2005f

institutional development impact (World Bank 2005a: 55–65). There is no reason to think that other major donors have performed any better (Lancaster 1999).

Failure, however, is not the same as 'no impact'. As we noted above the very extent and depth of external intervention is having a significant impact on politics in Ghana, and is generating a whole host of problems of coordination and policy implementation. Beyond these problems, it remains the case that projects that fail can nonetheless have significant effects on social, economic and political relationships. Individual development projects can skew the spending patterns and political accountability of local governments, just as they can shift or reinforce existing local social, political and economic structures. It has been argued that in many countries the myriad aid organizations at work 'have created a market for mostly young, under-employed local people able to communicate with foreigners', and that these people eventually assume 'a "spokesman" role' for the community which may be very different from their previous social position (Reusse 1999: 90). This points to the obvious, but often overlooked, fact that every aid project or programme in some way or another impacts upon its environment. It is just that at the moment we do not know very much about the impact of projects that 'fail' to achieve their objectives.[2] And even when external agencies are prepared to admit that projects don't work, they do not say what impact this failure has had.

The normative question

It should be clear from the above that the normative question – should the World Bank be trying to make liberalism real in developing countries – is more complicated than it might first appear. It was argued in the introduction that we ought to suspend judgement on this question until we have a better sense of what such a project of social transformation looks like in practice. Now that we have a better sense, it is hard to see how anyone could be unambiguously in favour of it. First, there is the obvious point that the World Bank has had limited success. Once we start to consider the possible costs of its actions, plus the unintended outcomes of failed projects, things start to look more complicated. It is one thing to say that you cannot make an omelette without breaking some eggs; it is quite another to break eggs by the dozen and make nothing but a terrible mess (Dunn 1979). It is important to stress too, that all this is driven by the seemingly boundless arrogance of Western agencies who believe themselves to be in possession of truth about social life for everyone. Even liberals should be wary of wholeheartedly endorsing this project as it manifest in the practices of the World Bank.

This argument – that the World Bank is not very good at social transformation – might be taken as an exhortation to do it better. And indeed, it seems very unlikely that the recognition of failures and missteps will deter the World Bank and other Western agencies from continuing their attempts at social transformation. They are, after all, committed to this project. To have an argument here, then, it is necessary to pose the normative question in a much broader way: something like, 'is liberalism true?' The answer to this question depends ultimately on how one views the possibilities of the 'view from nowhere'. That is, are the kinds of universal claims that liberalism rests on really possible? There are good reasons for thinking not. Above all, there are vast intellectual difficulties in showing that liberalism is more than a highly partial account of some of the practices and aspirations of some sections of Western societies (J. Gray 1986: 239). Despite what liberals claim, this is a very flimsy basis for messing around in people's lives.

This is not to say that there is no role for the World Bank in international politics, or indeed, in countries like Ghana. Nor, of course, is it to say that good outcomes will necessarily result from scaling back the World Bank's ambitions; the complexity of the development process makes any such claim hard to substantiate. And nor is it to cast doubt on the whole development enterprise (although there may be lots of criticisms one could make). It is only to say that we must be doubtful whether the World Bank should be pursuing a liberal project of transformation. More than anything else we should insist on some modesty: modesty about the basis of the liberal project, and modesty about what agencies like the World Bank should be doing.

Finally, for all the extensive discussion of liberalism and international relations, very little attention has been paid to the project of social transformation that has, so this book has argued, always been at the heart of liberal thought. From this perspective, liberalism in international relations is very far from the 'colossal fiasco' that Hoffman suggests (Hoffman 1986: 395). Instead, it has become embodied in and expressed through the political agency of numerous organizations. Far from being cowed or on the defensive, liberalism is triumphant. The real problem of liberalism and international relations is not that it has failed; it is that liberals want to remake the world in their own image.

Notes

Introduction

1 I owe this felicitous characterization of liberalism to Margaret Canovan (1990). See also Young (1995).
2 Countries make two kinds of contributions to the Bank. First, capital subscriptions to IBRD; the Bank never actually draws on these but they are used to back IBRD loans. Second, there are contributions to IDA, which the Bank then lends to the poorest developing countries.
3 In terms of the World Bank this obviously loaded phrase comes from Diane Stone and Christopher Wright, (Stone and Wright 2007). For a theoretically orientated argument see Neilson and Tierney (2003).
4 The phrase is from Cox (1986). For a discussion of this concept in the context of development see Boas and McNeil (2004).

1 Liberalism and social transformation

1 One could argue this drawing on the work of Quentin Skinner for example. See, Tully (1988b).
2 For an unabashed example see Franck (1997).
3 I am very much indebted to this article, not only in what follows, but for opening up an entire line of investigation into liberal thought.
4 This letter was written when Locke was in his late twenties, but as John Dunn has argued the scepticism it evinces remained a central theme throughout his life. See Dunn (1984).
5 The other examples included slavery and monopoly rights.

2 The World Bank, sovereignty and development

1 These were to France, the Netherlands, Denmark and Luxembourg. For more detail see Oliver (1975: 241–4).
2 It was only later that more sophisticated assessment techniques (discounted cash flows, internal rate of return) were utilized by the Bank. See Mason and Asher (1972: 241–2).

3 From structural adjustment to good governance

1 These recommendations were in line with Elliot Berg's previous work on African development. See for example, Berg (1971).
2 The role of powerful individuals within the Bank is discussed in Vetterlein (2007).
3 Lal wrote a famous polemic against what he understood as orthodox 'development economics' (Lal 1983).
4 The terms 'indigenous groups' or 'culture' are highly problematic. For now I will simply use them as they are used by the Bank.
5 This paper was withdrawn from circulation soon after it was originally released. Apart from its title, I see nothing in it which would be seen as unacceptable within the Bank today.

4 Governance, liberalism and social transformation

1 For a discussion of the Comprehensive Development Framework see Gulrajani (2007).

5 Transformation in practice

1 The project report specifies, among other things, the scale of the maps, their accuracy, the map content and even the contour lines to be used.

6 Sovereignty, development and the liberal project

1 For one case study see Jokinen (2004).
2 Unfortunately there is relatively little research on what we might call the local politics of project implementation.

Bibliography

Agarwala, R. (1990) 'Governance and institutional development in sub-Saharan Africa', in Corkery, J. and Bossuyt, J. (eds), *Governance and Institutional Development in Sub-Saharan Africa: Seminar Report*, Maastricht, European Centre for Development Policy Management.

Agarwala, R. and Schwartz, P. (1994) 'Sub-Saharan Africa: a long term perspective study', prepared for the World Bank Workshop on Participatory Development, May 1994.

Amsden, A. (1994) 'Why isn't the whole world experimenting with the East Asian model to develop? Review of the East Asian Miracle', *World Development* 22, 4: 627–33.

Arndt, H. (1987) *Economic Development: The History of an Idea*, Chicago, Chicago University Press.

Arneil, B. (1996) 'The wild Indian's venison: Locke's theory of property and English colonialism in America', *Political Studies* 44, 1: 60–74.

Aryeetey, E. (1994) 'Private investment under uncertainty in Ghana', *World Development* 22, 8: 1211–21.

Aryeetey, E. and Cox, A. (1997) 'Aid effectiveness in Ghana', in Carlsson, J., Smolokae G. and Van de Walle, N. (eds), *Foreign Aid In Africa: Learning from Country Experiences*, Uppsala, Nordiska Afrikainstitutet.

Ascher, W. (1983) 'New development approaches and the adaptability of international agencies: the case of the World Bank', *International Organization*, 37, 3: 415–39.

—— (1992) 'The World Bank and US Control', in Karns, M. and Mingst, K. (eds), *The United States and Multilateral Institution: Patterns of Changing Instrumentality and Influence*, London, Routledge.

Audi, R. (1998) 'A liberal theory of civic virtue', *Social Philosophy and Policy* 15, 1: 149–70.

Ayres, R. (1983) *Banking on the Poor: The World Bank and World Poverty*, Cambridge, MA, MIT Press.

Barkin, S. (1998) 'The evolution of the constitution of sovereignty and the emergence of human rights norms', *Millennium* 27, 2: 229–52.

Barkin, S. and Cronin, B. (1994) 'The state and the nation: changing norms and the rules of sovereignty in international relations', *International Organization* 48, 1: 107–30.

Barry, A., Osborne, T. and Rose, N. (eds) (1996) *Foucault and Political Reason: Liberalism, Neo-liberalism and Rationalities of Government*, London, University College London Press.

Barry, B. (1990) 'How not to defend liberal institutions', in Bruce Douglass, R., Mara, G. and Richardson, H. (eds), *Liberalism and the Good* New York, Routledge.

—— (2001) *Culture and Equality*, Cambridge, MA, Harvard University Press.

Bartleson, J. (1995) *A Genealogy of Sovereignty*, Cambridge, Cambridge University Press.

Batz, W. (1974) 'The historical anthropology of John Locke', *Journal of the History of Ideas* 35: 663–70.

Bazerman, C. (1993) 'Money talks: the rhetorical project of the Wealth of Nations', in Henderson, W., Dudley, T. and Blackhouse, R. (eds), *Economics and Language*, London, Routledge.

Beitz, C. (1979) *Political Theory and International Relations*, Princeton, Princeton University Press.

Benveniste, G. (1973) *The Politics of Expertise*, London, Croom Helm.

Berg, E. (1971) 'Structural transformation versus gradualism: recent economic development in Ghana and the Ivory Coast', in Foster, P. and Zoldberg, A. (eds), *Ghana and the Ivory Coast*, Chicago, University of Chicago Press.

Bergesen, H. and Lunde, L. (1999) *Dinosaurs or Dynamos? The United Nations and the World Bank at the Turn of the Century*, London, Earthscan.

Bhatnagar, B. and Williams, A. (eds) (1992a) *Participatory Development and the World Bank: Potential Directions for Change*, World Bank Discussion Paper, Washington DC, World Bank.

—— (1992b). 'Introduction', in Bhatnagar, B. and Williams, A. (eds) (1992a) *Participatory Development and the World Bank: Potential Directions for Change*, World Bank Discussion Paper, Washington DC, World Bank.

Biersteker, T. and Weber, C. (1996) 'The social construction of state sovereignty', in Biersteker, T. and Weber, C. (eds) (1996) *State Sovereignty as Social Construct*, Cambridge, Cambridge University Press.

Bitterman, H. (1971) 'Negotiation of the Articles of Agreement of the International Bank for Reconstruction and Development', *The International Lawyer* 5, 1: 59–88.

Black, E. (1963) *The Diplomacy of Economic Development*, Clinton, MA, The Colonial Press.

Blaug, M. (1980) *The Methodology of Economics: Or, How Economists Explain*, Cambridge, Cambridge University Press.

Boas, M. and McNeil, D. (2004) 'Power and ideas in multilateral institutions: towards an interpretive framework', in Boas, M. and McNeil, D (eds), *Global Institutions and Development: Framing the World?* London, Routledge.

Bratton, M. (1989) 'The politics of government–NGO relations in Africa', *World Development* 17, 4: 569–87.

Brett, E. (1993) 'Voluntary agencies and development organizations: theorizing the problem of efficiency and accountability', *Development and Change* 24, 2: 269–303.

Brinkerhoff, D. (1994) 'Institutional development in World Bank projects: analytical approaches and intervention design', *Public Administration and Development* 14, 1: 135–51.

Brown, B. (1992) *The United States and the Politicization of the World Bank: Issues of International Law and Policy*, London, Kegan Paul.

Burchell, G., Gordon, C. and Miller, P. (eds) (1991) *The Foucault Effect: Studies in Governmentality*, Brighton, Harvester Wheatsheaf.

Burley, A. (1993) 'Regulating the world: multilateralism, international law and the projection of the New Deal regulatory state', in Ruggie, J. (ed.), *Multilateralism Matters: The Theory and Praxis of an Institutional Form*, New York, Columbia University Press.

Burnell, P. (1991) *Charity, Politics and the Third World*, London, Harvester Wheatsheaf.

Burnham, J. (1994) 'Understanding the World Bank: a dispassionate analysis', in Bandow, D. and Vasquez, I. (eds), *Perpetuating Poverty: The World Bank, the IMF, and the Developing World*, Washington DC, Cato Institute.

Campos, E. and Lien, D. (1994) 'Institutions and the East Asian miracle: asymmetric information, rent-seeking, and the Deliberation Council', World Bank Policy Research Working Paper.

Canovan, M. (1990) 'On being economic with the truth: some liberal reflections', *Political Studies* 38, 1: 5–19.

Carlsson, J., Kohlin, G. and Ekbom, A. (1994) *The Political Economy of Evaluation: International Aid Agencies and the Effectiveness of Aid*, London, Macmillan.

Carlsson, J., Smolokae, G. and Van de Walle, N. (eds) (1997) *Foreign Aid In Africa: Learning from Country Experiences*, Uppsala, Nordiska Afrikainstitutet.

Carothers, T. (1994a) 'The democracy nostrum', *World Policy Journal*, Fall: 47–53.

—— (1994b) 'Democracy and human rights: policy allies or rivals?' *The Washington Quarterly* 17, 3: 109–20

Carrig, J. (2001) 'Liberal impediments to liberal education', *The Review of Politics* 63, 1: 41–76.

Cassen, R. (1986) *Does Aid Work?* Oxford, Clarendon.

Caulfield, C. (1997) *Masters of Illusion: The World Bank and the Poverty of Nations*, London, Macmillan.

Cernea, M. (1984) 'Can participation help development?' *Finance and Development* 21, 4: 41–4.

—— (1988) *Nongovernmental Organizations and Local Development*, World Bank Discussion Paper, Washington DC, World Bank.

Chalker, L. (1992) speech given to the Wilton Park Special Conference on 'Promoting Good Government in Africa', Steyning, England, January 1992.

Chambers, S. and Kopstein, J. (2001) 'Bad civil society', *Political Theory* 29, 6: 837–65.

Chambers, S. and Kymlicka, W. (eds) (2002) *Alternative Conceptions of Civil Society*, Princeton, Princeton University Press.

Charities Aid Foundation (1991) *Charity Trends*, 14th edn, Tonbridge, Charities Aid Foundation.

Charney, E. (1998) 'Political liberalism, deliberative democracy, and the public sphere', *American Political Science Review* 92, 1: 97–110.

Chenery, H. (1975) 'The structuralist approach to development policy', *American Economic Review* 65, 2: 310–15.

Chenery, H. and Stout, A. (1966) 'Foreign assistance and economic development', *American Economic Review* 56, 4:679–733.

Chenery, H., Ahluwalia, M., Bell, C., Duloy, J. and Jolly, R. (1974) *Redistribution with Growth*, Oxford, Oxford University Press for the World Bank.

Clark, J. (1991) *Democratizing Development: The Role of Voluntary Organizations*, London, Earthscan.

Clausen, A. (1982) 'A concluding perspective', in Fried, E. and Owen, H. (eds), *The Future of the World Bank*, Washington DC, Brookings Institution.

Coats, A. (1960) 'The first two decades of the American Economic Association', *American Economic Review* 50, 4: 556–74.

Cohen, J. and Arato, A. (1992) *The Political Thought of Civil Society*, Cambridge, MA, MIT Press.

Collier, P. (1991) 'From critic to secular god: a commentary on *Sub-Saharan African: From Crisis to Sustainable Growth*', *African Affairs* 90, 1: 111–17.

Cooper, F. (1997) 'Modernizing bureaucrats, backward Africans and the development concept', in Cooper, F. and Packard, R. (eds), *International Development and the Social Sciences: Essays on the History and Politics of Knowledge*, Berkeley, CA, University of California Press.

Cox, R. (1986) 'Social forces, states and world orders: beyond International Relations theory', in Keohane, R. (ed.), *Neorealism and its Critics*, New York, Columbia University Press.

Craig, D. and Porter, D. (2006) *Development Beyond Neoliberalism? Governance, Poverty Reduction and Political Economy*, London, Routledge.

Crane, B. and Finkle, J. (1981) 'Organizational impediments to development assistance: the World Bank's population program', *World Politics* 33, 4: 516–51.

Crawford, B. (1992) 'Time and money', in Bhatnagar, B. and Williams, A. (eds), *Participatory Development and the World Bank: Potential Directions for Change*, World Bank Discussion Paper, Washington DC, World Bank.

Critchlow, D. (1985) *The Brookings Institution 1916–1950: Expertise and the Public Interest in a Democratic Society*, Dekalb, IL, North West Illinois University Press.

Crocker, L. (1977) 'Equality, solidarity and Rawls' maximin', *Philosophy and Public Affairs*, 6, 3: 262–6.

Crook, R. (1994) 'Four years of the Ghana District Assemblies in operation: decentralisation, democratisation and administrative performance', *Public Administration and Development* 14, 4: 339–64.

Darlan, G. and Anani, K. (2006) *Delivering Services to the Poor: An Assessment of the Capacity to Deliver Education, Health and Water Services to Local Communities in Ghana*, Washington DC, World Bank Institute.

Davis, S. (1993) 'The World Bank and indigenous peoples', paper prepared for a panel discussion on Indigenous Peoples and Ethnic Minorities at the Denver Initiative Conference on Human Rights, University of Denver Law School, April 1993.

De Lusignan, G. (1986) 'The Bank's Economic Development Institute', *Finance and Development* 23, 2: 6–7.

Deng, F., Kimaro, S., Lyons, T., Rothchild, D. and Zartman, W. (1996) *Sovereignty as Responsibility: Conflict Management in Africa*, Washington DC, Brookings Institution.

Der Derian, J. (1987) *On Diplomacy*, Oxford, Blackwell.

Deudney, D. and Ikenberry, J. (1999) 'The nature and sources of liberal international order', *Review of International Studies* 25, 2: 179–96.

De Walle, A. (1997) *Famine Crimes: Politics and the Disaster Relief Industry in Africa*, London, James Currey.

Dia, M. (1991) 'Development and cultural values in Sub-Saharan Africa', *Finance and Development* 28, 4: 10–13.

—— (1994) 'Indigenous management practices: lessons for Africa's managers in the 1990s', in Serageldin, I. and Taboroff, J. (eds), *Culture and Development in Africa: Proceedings of an International Conference Held at the World Bank*, Washington DC, World Bank.

Donnelly, J. (1999) 'The social construction of international human rights', in Dunne, T. and Wheeler, N. (eds) (1999) *Human Rights in Global Politics*, Cambridge, Cambridge University Press.

Duffield, M. (2001a) *Global Governance and the New Wars: The Merging of Security and Development*, London, Zed.

—— (2001b) 'Governing the borderlands: decoding the power of aid', *Disasters* 25, 4: 308–20.

—— (2002) 'Social reconstruction and the radicalization of development: aid as a relation of liberal global governance', *Development and Change* 33, 5: 1049–72.

Dunn, J. (1979) *Western Political Theory in the Face of its Future*, Cambridge, Cambridge University Press.

—— (1984) 'The concept of "trust" in the politics of John Locke', in Rorty, R., Schneewind, J. and Skinner, Q. (eds), *Philosophy in History*, Cambridge, Cambridge University Press.

Dworkin, R. (1985a) 'Liberalism', in Dworkin, R., *A Matter of Principle*, Cambridge, MA, Harvard University Press.

—— (1985b) 'Why efficiency?' in Dworkin, R., *A Matter of Principle*, Cambridge, MA, Harvard University Press.

—— (1996) 'Objectivity and truth: you'd better believe it', *Philosophy and Public Affairs*, 25, 2: 87–139.

Ehdaie, J. (1994) 'Fiscal decentralization and the size of government: an extension with evidence from cross-country data', World Bank Policy Research Working Paper.

Eisenhardt, K. (1989) 'Agency theory: an assessment and review', *Academy of Management Review* 14, 1: 57–74.

Elbadawi, I., Ghura, D. and Uwujaren, G. (1992) 'Why structural adjustment has not succeeded in Sub-Saharan Africa', World Bank Policy Research Working Paper.

Emmerson, D. (1991) 'Capitalism, democracy and the World Bank: what is to be done?' in Deng, L., Kostner, M. and Young, C. (eds), *Democratization and Structural Adjustment in Africa in the 1990s*, Madison, WI, University of Wisconsin Madison African Studies Program.

Escobar, A. (1995) *Encountering Development: The Making and Unmaking of the Third World*, Princeton, Princeton University Press.

Esfahani, H. (1994) 'Regulations, institutions and economic performance', World Bank Policy Research Working Paper.

European Commission (2001) 'The European Union's role in promoting human rights and democratisation in third countries [COM(2001) 252 final, 8 May 2001]', Brussels, European Commission.

Feder, E. (1976) 'The new World Bank programme for the self-liquidation of the Third World peasantry', *The Journal of Peasant Studies* 3, 3: 343–54.

Feinberg, R. (1988) 'The changing relationship between the World Bank and the IMF', *International Organization* 42, 3: 545–60.

Fieldhouse, D. (1999) *The West and the Third World: Trade, Colonialism, Dependence and Development*, Oxford, Blackwell.

Finnemore, M. (1996) *National Interests in International Society*, Ithaca, Cornell University Press.

Foreign and Commonwealth Office (2005) *Sustainable Development Strategy*, London, FCO.

Foucault, M. (2001a) 'Omnes et singulatim: towards a criticism of "political reason"', in Faubian, J. (ed.) *Power: Essential Works of Foucault*, London, Penguin.

—— (2001b) 'Governmentality', in Faubian, J. (ed.) *Power: Essential Works of Foucault*, London, Penguin.

Fowler, A. (1993) 'Non-governmental Organizations as agents of democratization: an African perspective', *Journal of International Development* 5, 3: 325–39.

Franck, T. (1997) 'Is personal freedom a Western value?', *The American Journal of International Law*, 91, 4: 593–627.

Fraser, A. (2005) 'Poverty Reduction Strategy Papers: now who calls the shots?', *Review of African Political Economy*, 32, 104/5: 317–40.

Fried, E. and Owen, H. (eds) (1982) *The Future Role of the World Bank*, Washington DC, Brookings Institution.

Friedman, M. (1953) 'The methodology of positive economics', in Friedman, M., *Essays in Positive Economics*, Chicago, Chicago University Press.

Galston, W. (1982) 'Defending liberalism', *American Political Science Review* 76, 3: 621–29.

—— (1995) 'Two concepts of liberalism', *Ethics* 105, 3: 516–34.

Gary, I. (1996) 'Confrontation, co-operation or co-option: NGOs and the Ghanaian state during structural adjustment', *Review of African Political Economy* 23, 68: 149–68.

Gauthier, D. (1986) *Morals by Agreement*, Oxford, Oxford University Press.

George, S. (1976) *How the Other Half Dies: The Real Reasons for World Hunger*, London, Penguin.

George, S. and Sabelli, F. (1994) *Faith and Credit: The World Bank's Secular Empire*, London, Penguin.

Gibbon, P. (1993) 'The World Bank and the new politics of aid', *European Journal of Development Research* 5, 1: 35–62.

Gilpin, R. (1987) *The Political Economy of International Relations*, Princeton, NJ, Princeton University Press.

Goldman, M. (2000) 'The power of World Bank knowledge', briefing, Bretton Woods Project.

Goldsmith, A. (2005) 'How good must governance be?', paper prepared for 'The Quality of Government: What is it, How to Get it, Why it Matters' conference, Göteborg University, Sweden, November 2005.

Gong, G. (1984) *The Standard of 'Civilisation' in International Society*, Oxford, Clarendon.

Goodin R. and Reeve, A. (eds) (1989) *Liberal Neutrality*, London, Routledge.

Gordon, C. (1991) 'Governmental rationality: an introduction', in Burchell, G., Gordon, C. and Miller, P. (eds), *The Foucault Effect: Studies in Governmentality*, London, Harvester Wheatsheaf.

Government of Japan (1999) Ministry of Foreign Affairs, *ODA Annual Report 1999*, Tokyo, Government of Japan.

Grant, R. (1988) 'Locke's political anthropology and Lockean individualism', *Journal of Politics* 50, 1: 42–63.

Gray, A. (1998) 'Development policy – development protest: The World Bank, indigenous peoples and NGOs', in Fox, J. and Brown, D. (eds), *The Struggle for Accountability: The World Bank, NGOs, and Grassroots Movements*, Cambridge, MA, MIT Press.

Gray, C., Khadiagala, L. and Moore, R. (1990) *Institutional Development Work in the Bank: A Review of 84 Bank Projects*, Policy Research and External Affairs Working Paper, Washington DC, World Bank.

Gray, J. (1986) *Liberalisms*, Milton Keynes, Open University Press.

Greenwald, B. and Stiglitz, J. (1986) 'Externalities in economies with imperfect information and incomplete markets', *Quarterly Journal of Economics* 101, 2: 229–64.

Gulrajani, N. (2007) 'The art of fine balances: the challenge of institutionalizing the Comprehensive Development Framework inside the World Bank', in Stone, D. and Wright, C. (eds), *The World Bank and Governance: A Decade of Reform and Reaction*, London, Routledge.

Gwin, C. (1997) 'US relations with the World Bank: 1945–1992', in Kapur, D., Lewis, J. and Webb, R. (eds), *The World Bank: Its First half Century*, vol. 2, Washington DC, Brookings Institution Press.

Habermas, J. (1989) *The Structural Transformation of the Public Sphere: An Inquiry into a Category of Bourgeois Society*, trans. Thomas Berger, Cambridge, MA, MIT Press.

Harrison, G. (2004) *The World Bank and Africa: The Construction of Governance States*, London, Routledge.

Harrold, P. (2000) 'Setting the context of civil society engagement', in Mackay, K. and Gariba, S. (eds), *The Role of Civil Society in Assessing Public Sector Performance in Ghana*, Washington DC, World Bank.

Harsanyi, J. (1982) 'Morality and the theory of rational behaviour', in Sen, A. and Williams, B. (eds), *Utilitarianism and Beyond*, Cambridge, Cambridge University Press.

Haskell, T. (1978) 'Professionalization as cultural reform', *Humanities in Society* 1, 2: 103–14.

——— (ed) (1984) *The Authority of Experts: Studies in History and Theory*, Bloomington, IN, Indiana University Press.

Hawthorn, G. and Seabright, P. (1993) 'Where Westphalia fails: the conditionality of the International Financial Institutions and national sovereignty', draft paper, Cambridge, August 1993.

Hayter, T. and Watson, C. (1985) *Aid: Reality and Rhetoric*, London, Pluto.

Helleiner, G. (1980) *International Economic Disorder: Essays in North–South Relations*, London, Macmillan.

Higgins, R. (1994) *Problems and Processes: International Law and How We Use It*, Oxford, Clarendon.

Hindess, B. (2002a) 'Neo-Liberal citizenship', *Citizenship Studies* 6, 2: 127–43.

—— (2002b) 'Metropolitan liberalism and colonial autocracy', in Hillier, J. and Rooksby, E. (eds), *Habitus: A Sense of Place*, London, Ashgate.

—— (2004) 'Liberalism: what's in a name?' in Larner, W. and Walter, W. (eds), *Global Governmentality: Governing International Space*, London, Routledge.

Hirschman, A. (1977) *The Passions and the Interests: Political Arguments for Capitalism Before its Triumph*, Princeton, Princeton University Press.

—— (1982) 'Rival interpretations of market society: civilizing, destructive or feeble', *Journal of Economic Literature* 20: 1463–84.

Hodd, M. (1987) 'Africa, the IMF, and the World Bank', *African Affairs* 86, 344: 331–42.

Hoffman, S. (1986) 'Liberalism and international affairs', in Hoffman, S., *Janus and Minerva: Essays in the Theory and Practice of International Politics*, Boulder, CO, Westview.

Howe, G. (1982) 'The International Monetary Fund and the World Bank: the British approach', *International Affairs* 58, 2: 199–209.

Hundert, E. (1977) 'Market society and meaning in Locke's political philosophy', *Journal of the History of Philosophy* 15, 1: 33–44.

Hurd, D. (1990) Speech given to Overseas Development Institute, London, June 1990.

Hussi, P., Murphy, J., Lindberg, O. and Brenneman, L. (1993) *The Development of Cooperatives and Other Rural Organizations: The Role of the World Bank*, World Bank Technical Paper, Washington DC, World Bank.

International Bank for Reconstruction and Development (1951) *Sixth Annual Report*, Washington DC, IBRD.

International Commission on Intervention and State Sovereignty (2001) *Responsibility to Protect*, Ottawa, International Development Research Centre.

Israel, A. (1987) *Institutional Development: Incentives to Performance*, Baltimore, MD, Johns Hopkins University Press for the World Bank.

Jackson, R. (1993) *Quasi-States: Sovereignty, International Relations and the Third World*, Cambridge, Cambridge University Press.

Jahn, B. (2005) 'Kant, Mill, and illiberal legacies in international affairs', *International Organisation* 59, 4: 177–207.

Jayarajah, C. and Branson, W. (1995) *Structural and Sectoral Adjustment: World Bank Experience, 1980–1992*, Operations Evaluation Study, Washington DC, World Bank.

Jaycox, E. (1995) 'Capacity building: the missing link in African development', address to the African–American Institute Conference, 'African Capacity Building: Effective and Enduring Partnerships', Reston, VA, May 1995.

Jeffries, R. (1989) 'Ghana: the political economy of personal rule', in Cruise O'Brien, D., Dunn, J. and Rathbone, R. (eds), *Contemporary West African States*, Cambridge, Cambridge University Press.

Johnson, J. and Wasty, S. (1993) *Borrower Ownership of Adjustment Programs and the Political Economy of Reform*, World Bank Discussion Paper, Washington DC, World Bank.

Johnson, S. (1996) *Education and Training of Accountants in Sub-Saharan Anglophone Africa*, World Bank Technical paper, Washington DC, World Bank.

Jokinen, J. (2004) 'Balancing between East and West: the Asian Development Bank's policy on good governance', in Boas, M. and McNeil, D. (eds), *Global Institutions and Development: Framing the World?* London, Routledge.

Kadish, A. and Tribe, K. (eds) (1993) *The Market for Political Economy: The Advent of Economics in British University Culture, 1850–1905*, London, Routledge.

Kant, I. (1970) 'On the common saying "This may be true in theory but it does not apply in practice', *Kant's Political Writings*, Cambridge, Cambridge University Press.

—— (1997) *Groundwork of the Metaphysics of Morals*, Cambridge, Cambridge University Press.

Kapur, D. (2002) 'The changing anatomy of governance of the World Bank', in Pincus, J. and Withers, G. (eds), *Reinventing the World Bank*, Ithaca, Cornell University Press.

Kasanga, K. and Kotey, N. (2001) *Land Management in Ghana: Building on Tradition and Modernity*, London, International Institute for Environment and Development.

Kateb, G. (1994) 'Notes on Pluralism', *Social Research* 61, 3: 511–37.

Kaufmann, D. (2004) 'Corruption, governance and security: challenges for the rich countries and the World', in World Economic Forum, *Global Competitiveness Report 2004/2005*, Geneva, World Economic Forum.

Kaufmann, D., Kraay, A. and Mastruzzi, M. (2005a) 'Governance Matters IV: Governance Indicators for 1996–2004', Policy Research Working paper, Washington DC, World Bank.

—— (2005b) 'Governance matters IV: new data, new challenges', synthesis paper, Washington DC, World Bank.

Keane, J. (1998) *Civil Society: Old Images, New Visions*, Cambridge, Polity.

Keck, M. and Sikkink, K. (1998) *Activists Beyond Borders: Advocacy Networks in International Politics*, Ithaca, Cornell University Press.

Kenny, C. and Williams, D. (2001) 'What do we know about economic growth? Or, why don't we know very much', *World Development* 29, 1: 1–22.

Keohane, R. and Nye, J. (eds) (1972) *Transnational Relations and World Politics*, Cambridge, MA, Harvard University Press.

Killick, T. (1978) *Development Economic in Action: A Study of Economic Policies in Ghana*, London, Heineman.

Klitgaard, R. (1995) *Institutional Adjustment and Adjusting to Institutions*, World Bank Discussion Paper, Washington DC, World Bank.

Knack, S. (2000) 'Aid dependence and the quality of governance: A cross-country empirical analysis', World Bank Research Paper, Washington DC, World Bank.

Krasner, S. (1999) *Sovereignty: Organized Hypocrisy*, Princeton, Princeton University Press.

Krueger, A. (1974) 'The political economy of the rent-seeking society', *American Economic Review* 64, 3: 291–303.

—— (1986) 'Changing perspectives on development economics and World Bank research', Development Policy Review 4, 3: 195–210.

Krueger, A., Schiff, M. and Valdes, A. (eds) (1991/1992) *The Political Economy of Agricultural Pricing*, 5 vols, Baltimore, MD, Johns Hopkins University Press for the World Bank.

Kymlicka, W. (1989) 'Liberal individualism and liberal neutrality', *Ethics*, 99: 883–905.

—— (1991) *Liberalism, Community and Culture*, Oxford, Clarendon.

—— (1992) 'The rights of minority cultures: Reply to Kukathas', *Political Theory*, 20, 1: 140–6.

Lal, D. (1983) *The Poverty of 'Development Economics'*, London, IEA.

—— (1984) *The Political Economy of the Predatory State*, World Bank Development Research Department Paper.

—— (1987) 'The political economy of economic liberalization', *World Bank Economic Review* 1, 2: 272–99.

Lamb, G. (1987) *Managing Economic Policy Change: Institutional Dimensions*, World Bank Discussion Paper, Washington DC, World Bank.

Lamb, G. and Muller, L. (1982) *Control, Accountability and Incentives in a Successful Development Institution: The Kenya Tea Authority*, World Bank Staff Working Paper, Washington DC, World Bank.

Lancaster, C. (1999) *Aid to Africa: So Much to do, So Little Done*, Chicago, University of Chicago Press.

Landell-Mills, P. (1992a) 'Governance, civil society and empowerment in Sub-Saharan Africa', paper prepared for the Annual Conference of the Society for the Advancement of Socio-economics, May 1992.

—— (1992b) 'Creating transparency, predictability and an enabling environment for private enterprise', paper presented at a Wilton Park Conference on 'Promoting Good Governance in Africa', Steyning, England, January 1992.

Larson, M. (1977) *The Rise of Professionalism: A Sociological Analysis*, Berkeley, University of California Press.

Latham, R. (1997) *The Liberal Moment: Modernity, Security, and the Making of Postwar International Order*, New York, Columbia University Press.

Leith, C. and Lofchie, M. (1993) 'The political economy of adjustment in Ghana', in Bates, R. and Kreuger, A. (eds), *Political and Economic Interactions in Economic Policy: Evidence from Eight Countries*, Oxford, Blackwell.

Le Pestre, P. (1986) 'A problematique for international organizations', *International Social Science Journal* 107: 127–38.

—— (1989) *The World Bank and the Environmental Challenge*, London, Associated University Press.

Lindauer, D. and Nunberg, B. (eds) (1994) *Rehabilitating Government: Pay and Employment Reform*, Washington DC, World Bank.

Lipton, M. and Toye, J. (1990) *Does Aid Work in India? A Country Case Study of Overseas Development Assistance*, London, Routledge.

Locke, J. (1976) *Essay Concerning Human Understanding*, London, Dent.

—— (1989) *Two Treatise on Government*, London, Everyman.

—— (1993a) 'Letter to Tom', in *Political Writings* (ed.) David Wootton, London, Penguin.

—— (1993b) 'Credit, disgrace', in *Political Writings* (ed.) David Wootton, London, Penguin.

—— (1993c) 'Philanthropy or The Christian Philosophers', in *Political Writings* (ed.) David Wootton, London, Penguin.

—— (1993d) 'An Essay Concerning Toleration', in *Political Writings* (ed.) David Wootton, London, Penguin.

—— (1993e) 'Draft of a Representation Containing a Scheme of Methods for the Employment of the Poor. Proposed by Mr. Locke', in *Political Writings* (ed.) David Wootton, London, Penguin.

—— (1996) *Some Thoughts Concerning Education and of the Conduct of the Understanding*, (eds) Grant, R. and Tarcov, N., Indianapolis IN, Hackett.

Lovejoy, A. (1936) *The Great Chain of Being: A Study of an Idea*, Cambridge, MA, Harvard University Press.

Lukes, S. (1973) *Individualism*, Oxford, Blackwell.

Maier, C. (1978) 'The politics of productivity: Foundations of American international economic policy after World War II', in Katzenstein, P. (ed.), *Between Power and Plenty: Foreign Economic Policies of Advanced Industrial States*, Madison, WI, University of Wisconsin Press.

Marshall, A. (1920) *Principles of Economics*, London, Macmillan.

Mason E. and Asher, R. (1972) *The World Bank Since Bretton Woods*, Washington DC, Brookings Institution.

Mayall, J. (1989) '1789 and the liberal theory of international society', *Review of International Studies* 15; 297–307.

McKitterick, N. (1986) 'The World Bank and the McNamara legacy', *The National Interest* 4, Summer: 45–52.

Mehta, U. (1992) *The Anxiety of Freedom: Imagination and Individuality in Locke's Political Thought*, Ithaca, Cornell University Press.

Mendus, S. (1989) *Toleration and the Limits of Liberalism*, London, Macmillan.

Mikesell, R. (1972) 'The emergence of the World Bank as a development institution', in Acheson, K., Chant, J. and Prachowny, M. (eds), *Bretton Woods Revisited*, London, Macmillan.

Mill, J. S. (1972) *Utilitarianism, on Liberty, and Considerations on Representative Government*, London, Dent.

—— (1973) 'A Few Words on Non-intervention', in Himmelfarb, G. (ed.) *Essays on Politics and Culture*, Gloucester, MA, Peter Smith.

—— (1976) *On Liberty*, London, Penguin.

—— (1990) 'Memorandum of the improvements in the Administration of India during the last Thirty years'[1858], in Robson, J., Moir, M. and Moir, Z. (eds) *John Stuart Mill Collected Works Vol XXX: Writings on India*, London, Routledge.

Mitterrand, F. (1990) interview, *Le Monde* 20 June 1990.

Moir, M. (1990) 'Introduction', in Robson, J., Moir, M. and Moir Z. (eds) *John Stuart Mill Collected Works Vol XXX: Writings on India*, London, Routledge.

Morton, J. (1996) *The Poverty of Nations: The Aid Dilemma at the Heart of Africa*, London, Tauris.

Mosley, P., Harrigan, J. and Toye, J. (1991) *Aid and Power: The World Bank and Policy-based Lending*, 2 vols, London, Routledge.

Nagel, T. (1986) *The View From Nowhere*, Oxford, Oxford University Press.

—— (1991) *Equality and Partiality*, Oxford, Oxford University Press.

Naim, M. (1994) 'The World Bank: its role, governance and organizational culture', Bretton Woods Commission, in Bretton Woods Commission, *Bretton Woods: Looking to the Future*, Washington DC, Bretton Woods Commission.

Neilson, D. and Tierney, M. (2003) 'Delegation to international organizations: agency theory and World Bank environmental reform', *International Organization*, 57, 2: 241–76.

NGO Working Group on the World Bank (1989) 'Position paper of the NGO Working Group on the World Bank', Geneva, December 1989.

North, D. (1994) Speech given at the World Bank, 18 February 1994.

Nunberg, B. and Nellis, J. (1995) *Civil Service Reform and the World Bank*, World Bank Discussion Paper, Washington DC, World Bank.

OECD (1988) *Voluntary Aid for Development: The Role of Non-governmental Organizations*, Paris, OECD.

OECF (1991) 'Issues related to the World Bank's approach to structural adjustment – proposal from a major partner', OECF Occasional Paper no.1, October 1991.

Oliver, R. (1975) *International Economic Co-operation and the World Bank*, London, Macmillan.

Onuf, N. (1998) *The Republican Legacy in International Thought*, Cambridge, Cambridge University Press.

Oquaye, M. (1995) 'Decentralisation and development: the Ghanian case under the Provisional National Defense Council (PNDC)', *Journal of Commonwealth and Comparative Politics* 33, 2: 209–39.

Osiander, A. (1994) *The States System of Europe, 1640–1990: Peacemaking and the Conditions of International Stability*, Oxford, Clarendon.

Parekh, B. (1995) 'Liberalism and colonialism', in Nederveen, J. and Parekh, B. (eds), *The Decolonisation of Imagination*, London, Zed.

Parfitt, T. (1993) 'Which African agenda for the nineties? The ECA/World Bank alternatives', Journal of International Development 5, 1: 93–106.

Patrick, S. (2006) *Weak States and Global Threats: Assessing Evidence of "Spillovers"*, Centre for Global Development Working Paper 73, Washington DC, CGD.

Paul, E., Miller, F. and Paul, J. (eds) (2005) *Natural Rights Liberalism from Locke to Nozick*, Cambridge, Cambridge University Press.

Paul, S. (1987a) *Community Participation in Development Projects: The World Bank Experience*, World Bank Discussion Paper, Washington DC, World Bank.

—— (1987b) 'Community participation in World Bank projects', *Finance and Development* 24, 4: 20–3.

—— (1987c) 'Private Sector Assessment: a pilot exercise in Ghana', Policy Planning and Research Working Paper, November 1987.

—— (1990) *Institutional Development in World Bank Projects: A Cross-Sectoral Review*, Policy Research and External Affairs Working Paper, Washington DC, World Bank.

—— (1991) *Strengthening Public Service Accountability: A Conceptual Framework*, World Bank Discussion Paper, Washington DC, World Bank.

—— (1992) 'Accountability in public services: exit, voice and control', *World Development* 20, 7: 1047–60.

Payer, C. (1982) *The World Bank: A Critical Analysis*, New York, Monthly Review Press.

Peacock, A. and Rowley, C. (1972) 'Pareto optimality and the political economy of liberalism', *Journal of Political Economy* 80, 3: 476–90.

Picciotto, R. (1995) *Putting Institutional Economics to Work: From Participation to Governance*, World Bank Discussion Paper, Washington DC, World Bank.

Please, S. (1984) *The Hobbled Giant: Essays on the World Bank*, Boulder, CO, Westview.

—— (1990) 'Governance and institutional development in Sub-Saharan Africa', in Corkery, J. and Bossuyt, J. (eds), *Governance and Institutional Development in Sub-Saharan Africa: Seminar Report*, Maastricht, European Centre for Development Policy Management.

Pogge, T. (2000) *World Poverty and Human Rights: Cosmopolitan Reasons and Reforms*, Cambridge, Polity.

Poggi, G. (1990) *The State: Its Nature, Development and Prospects*, Stanford, Stanford University Press.

Polak, J. (1994) 'The World Bank and the IMF: the future of their coexistence', in Bretton Woods Commission, *Bretton Woods: Looking to the Future*. Washington DC, Bretton Woods Commission.

Polanyi, K. (1957) *The Great Transformation: The Political and Economic Origins of Our Time*, Boston, MA, Beacon.

Portfolio Management Task Force (1992) 'Effective implementation: key to development impact', September 1992.

Putnam, R. (1995) *Bowling Alone: The Collapse and Revival of American Community*, New York, Simon and Schuster.

Rathbone, R. (2000) *Nkrumah and the Chiefs: The Politics of Chieftaincy in Ghana 1951–1960*, London, James Currey.

Rawls, J. (1971) *A Theory of Justice*, Oxford, Oxford University Press.

—— (1985) 'Justice as fairness: political not metaphysical', *Philosophy and Public Affairs* 14, 3: 223–51.

—— (1993a) *Political Liberalism*, New York, Columbia University Press.

—— (1993b) 'The law of peoples', in Shute, S. and Hurley, S. (eds), *On Human Rights: The Oxford Amnesty Lectures 1993*, New York, Basic Books.

Reusse, E. (1999) *Interventionist Paradigms and the Ills of Aid*, Munich, Olzog.

Reus-Smit, C. (1999) *The Moral Purpose of the State: Culture, Social Identity, and Institutional Identity in International Relations*, Princeton, Princeton University Press.

Rhee, Y. (1985) *A Framework for Export Policy and Administration*, World Bank Staff Working Paper, Washington DC, World Bank.

Rice, C. (2005) 'A conversation with Condoleeza Rice', *The American Interest* Autumn: 47–50.

Rich, B. (1994) *Mortgaging the Earth: The World Bank, Environmental Impoverishment and the Crisis of Development*, London, Earthscan.

Robinson, M. (1991) 'An uncertain partnership: the Overseas Development Administration and the voluntary sector in the 1980s', in Bose, A. and Burnell, P. (eds), *Britain's Overseas Aid Since 1979: Between Idealism and Self-interest*, Manchester, Manchester University Press.

Rorty, R. (1983) 'Postmodern bourgeois liberalism', *The Journal of Philosophy* 80, 10: 583–9.

—— (1993) 'Human rights, rationality, and sentimentality', in Shute, S. and Hurley, S. (eds), *On Human Rights: The Oxford Amnesty Lectures 1993*, New York, Basic Books.

Rose, N. (1996) 'Governing "advanced" liberal democracies', in Barry, A., Osborne, T. and Rose, N. (eds), *Foucault and Political Reason: Liberalism, Neo-liberalism and Rationalities of Government*, London, University College London Press.

Rosenberg, N. (1960) 'Some institutional aspects of the Wealth of Nations', *Journal of Political Economy* 68, 6: 557–70.

Rosenblum, N. (1989) *Liberalism and the Moral Life*, Cambridge, MA, Harvard University Press.

Rothschild, D. (1985) 'The Rawlings revolution in Ghana: pragmatism with populist rhetoric', *CSIS Africa Notes* 42, 2 May 1985.

Rowat, M., Malik, W. and Dakolias, M. (eds) (1995) *Judicial Reform in Latin America and the Caribbean: Proceedings of the World Bank Conference*, World Bank Technical Paper, Washington DC, World Bank.

Ruggie, J. (1982) 'International regimes, transaction, and change: embedded liberalism in the Postwar economic order', *International Organization* 36, 2: 195–231

—— (1986) 'Continuity and transformation in the world polity: toward a Neorealist synthesis', in Keohane, R. (ed.), *Neorealism and its Critics*, New York, Columbia University Press.

—— (1998) 'Introduction: what makes the world hang together? Neo-utilitarianism and the Social Constructivist Challenge', in Ruggie, J., *Constructing the World Polity: Essays on International Institutionalization*, London, Routledge.

Salkever, S. (1977) 'Freedom, participation, happiness', *Political Theory* 5, 3: 391–413.

—— (1990) '"Lopp'd and bound": how liberal theory obscures the goods of liberal practice', in Bruce Douglass, R., Mara, G. and Richardson, H. (eds), *Liberalism and the Good*, New York, Routledge.

Salmen, L. (1987) 'Listening to the people', *Finance and Development* 24, 2: 36–9.

Salmen, L. and Paige Eaves, A. (1991) 'Interactions between Nongovernmental Organizations, governments, and the World Bank: evidence from Bank projects', in Paul, S. and Israel, A. (eds), *Nongovernmental Organizations and the World Bank: Cooperation for Development*, Washington DC, World Bank.

Sandel, M. (1982) *Liberalism and the Limits of Justice*, Cambridge, Cambridge University Press.

Sandstrom, S. (1994) 'Participation and sustainable development: applying the lessons of experience', Keynote Address to the Annual Conference of the International Association of Public Participation Practitioners, Washington DC, September 1994.

Schultz, T. (1964) *Transforming Traditional Agriculture*, New Haven, Yale University Press.

Seligman, A. (1992) *Civil Society*, New York, Free Press.

Serageldin, I. (1990) 'Governance, democracy and the World Bank in Africa', discussion paper delivered at a World Bank Legal Department Staff meeting, 30 November 1990.

—— (1995) *Nurturing Development: Aid and Cooperation in Today's Changing World*, Washington DC, World Bank.

Serageldin, I. and Taboroff, J. (eds) (1994) *Culture and Development in Africa: Proceedings of an International Conference held at the World Bank*, Washington DC, World Bank.

Shihata, I. (1991a) 'The World Bank and "governance" issues in its borrowing countries', in Shihata, I., *The World Bank in a Changing World: Selected Essays*, Dordrecht, Martinus Nijhoff.

—— (1991b) 'The World Bank and human rights', in Shihata, I., *The World Bank in a Changing World: Selected Essays*, Dordrecht, Martinus Nijhoff.

—— (1992) 'The World Bank and Non-Governmental Organizations', *Cornell International Law Journal* 2, 3: 623–44.

Silverman, J. (1992) *Public Sector Decentralization: Economic Policy and Sector Investment Programs*, World Bank Technical Paper, Washington DC, World Bank.

Smith, A. (1976) *An Enquiry into the Nature and Causes of the Wealth of Nations*, Glasgow Edition, Oxford, Oxford University Press.

—— (1978) *Lectures on Jurisprudence*, Glasgow Edition, Oxford, Oxford University Press.

—— (1982) *The Theory of Moral Sentiments*, Glasgow Edition, Oxford, Oxford University Press.

Stein, H. and Nafziger, W. (1991) 'Structural adjustment, human needs, and the World Bank agenda', *The Journal of Modern African Studies* 29, 1: 173–89.

Stern E. (1991), 'Evolution and lessons of adjustment lending', in Thomas, T., Chibber, A., Dailami, M. and de Melo, J. (eds), *Restructuring Economies in Distress: Policy Reform and the World Bank*, Oxford, Oxford University Press for the World Bank.

Stern N. and Ferreira, F. (1997) 'The World Bank as "intellectual actor"', in Kapur, D., Lewis, J. and Webb, R. (eds), *The World Bank: Its First half Century*, vol. 2, Washington DC, Brookings Institution Press.

Stevaluk, C. and Thompson, A. (1993) 'Approaches for World Bank staff on working with Nongovernmental Organizations', Discussion Draft, June 1993.

Stiglitz, J. (1989) 'Markets, market imperfections and development', *American Economic Review* 79, 20: 197–303.

—— (1996) 'Some lessons from the East Asian Miracle', *The World Bank Research Observer* 11, 2: 151–77.

Stiglitz, J. (1997) 'An agenda for development in the twenty-first century', Address to the Annual Bank Conference on Development Economics, Washington DC, 30 April and 1 May 1997.

—— (1998) 'Towards a new paradigm for development: strategies, policies and processes', Prebisch Lecture, Geneva, UNCTAD, October 1998.

Stone, D. and Wright, C. (2007) 'The currency of change: World Bank lending and learning in the Wolfensohn era', in Stone, D. and Wright, C. (eds), *The World Bank and Governance: A Decade of Reform and Reaction*, London, Routledge.

Taylor, C. (1990) 'Modes of civil society', *Public Culture* 3, 1: 119–32.

—— (1995) 'Invoking civil society', in Taylor, C., *Philosophical Arguments*, Cambridge, MA, Harvard University Press.

Thomas, G. and Lauderdale, P. (1988) 'State authority and national welfare programs in the world system context' *Sociological Forum* 3, 3: 383–99.

Toye, J. (1987) *Dilemmas of Development*, Oxford, Blackwell.

—— (1991) 'Ghana', in Mosley, P., Harrigan, J. and Toye, J., *Aid and Power: The World Bank and Policy-based Learning* vol. 2, London, Routledge.

—— (1992) 'Interest group politics and the implementation of adjustment policies in Sub-Saharan Africa', *Journal of International Development* 4, 2:183–97.

Tribe, K. (1991) 'Political economy to economics via commerce: the evolution of British academic Economics 1860–1920', in Wagner, P., Wittrock, B. and Whitely, R. (eds), *Discourses on Society: The Shaping of the Social Science Disciplines*, Dordrecht, Kluwer Academic Publishers.

Tully, J. (1988a) 'Governing conduct', in Leites, E. (ed.) (1988) *Conscience and Casuistry in Early Modern Europe*, Cambridge, CUP.

Tully, J. (ed) (1988b) *Quentin Skinner and His Critics*, Princeton, Princeton University Press.

Ullmann-Margalit, E. (1999) 'The invisible hand and the cunning of reason', in Avnon, D. and De-Shalit, A. (eds), *Liberalism and its Practice*, London, Routledge.

UNDP (1998) *UNDP and Governance*, New York, UNDP/Management and Governance Network.

USAID (1991) 'Democracy and governance paper', November 1991, Washington DC.

—— (2003) *Foreign Aid in the National Interest: Promoting Freedom, Security and Opportunity*, Washington DC, USAID.

—— (2005) *At Freedom's Frontiers: A Democracy and Governance Strategic Framework*, Washington DC, USAID.

Van de Sand, K. and Mohs, R. (1992) 'Making German aid more credible', *Development and Co-operation* 1: 4–5.

Vaudel, R. (1991) 'A public choice view of international organization', in Vaudel, R. and Willet, T. (eds), *The Political Economy of International Organizations: A Public Choice Approach*, Boulder, CO, Westview.

Vetterlein, A. (2007) 'Change in international organizations: innovation or adaptation: a comparison of the World Bank and the International Monetary Fund', in Stone, D. and Wright, C. (eds), *The World Bank and Governance: A Decade of Reform and Reaction*, London, Routledge.

Viner, J. (1958) 'Adam Smith and laissez-faire', in Viner, J. (1958) *The Long View and the Short*, Glencoe, IL, Free Press.

Vogel, U. (1988) 'When the land belonged to all: the land question in eighteenth-century justifications of private property', *Political Studies* 36, 1: 102–22.

Volpa, A. (1992) 'Conceiving a public: ideas and society in eighteenth-century Europe', *The Journal of Modern History* 64: 79–116.

Wade, R. (1996) 'Japan, the World Bank, and the art of paradigm maintenance: The East Asian Miracle in political perspective', *New Left Review* 217: 3–36.

—— (2001) 'Showdown at the World Bank', *New Left Review*, No. 7: 124–37.

—— (2004) 'The World Bank and the environment', in Boas, M. and McNeil, D. (eds), *Global Institutions and Development: Framing the World?* London, Routledge

Waldron, J. (ed.) (1984) *Theories of Rights*, Oxford, Oxford University Press.

—— (1987) 'The theoretical foundations of liberalism', *Philosophical Quarterly* 37, 147: 127–50.

Walker, R. (1993) *Inside/Outside: International Relations as Political Theory*, Cambridge, Cambridge University Press.

Weaver, C. and Leiteritz, R. (2005) '"Our poverty is a world full of dreams": reforming the World Bank', *Global Governance* 11: 369–88.

White House (2002) *National Security Strategy of the United States of America*, Washington DC, The White House.

Whitfield, L. (2005) 'Trustees of development from conditionality to governance: Poverty Reduction Strategy Papers in Ghana', *Journal of Modern African Studies* 43, 4: 641–64.

Williams, D. (1996) 'Governance and the discipline of development', *European Journal of Development Research* 8, 2: 157–77.

Williams, D. (2003) 'Managing sovereignty: the World Bank and development in Sub-Saharan Africa', *Mondes en Development* 31, 3: 5–22.

Williams, D. and Young, T. (1994) 'Governance, the World Bank and liberal theory', *Political Studies* 42, 1: 84–100.

Winch, D. (1983) 'Science and the legislator: Adam Smith and after', *The Economic Journal*, 93: 501–29.

Wittrock, B., Wagner, P. and Wollman, H. (1991) 'Social science and the modern state: policy knowledge and political institutions in Western Europe and the United States', in Wagner, P., Weiss, C., Wittrock, B. and Wollman, H. (eds), *Social Sciences and Modern States: National Experiences and Theoretical Cross-roads*, Cambridge, Cambridge University Press.

Wolfensohn, J. (1999) 'A proposal for a Comprehensive Development Framework', paper, 21 January 1999.

—— (2004) Address to Board of Governors of the World Bank at the Joint IMF/ World Bank meetings, 3 October 2004.

Woods, N. (2006) *The Globalizers: The IMF, the World Bank, and their Borrowers*, Cornell, Cornell University Press.

World Bank (1981) *Accelerated Development in Sub-Saharan Africa: An Agenda for Action*, World Bank, Washington DC.

—— (1982) Operational Manual Statement 2.34.

World Bank (1983a) *World Development Report 1983*, Washington DC, World Bank.

—— (1983b) *Sub-Saharan Africa: A Progress Report on Development Prospects and Programs*, Washington DC, World Bank.

—— (1984) *Towards Sustained Development in Sub-Saharan Africa*, Washington DC, World Bank.

—— (1985) 'New research priorities', World Bank Research News 6, 1.

—— (1986a) *Financing Adjustment with Growth in Sub-Saharan Africa: 1986–1990*, Washington DC, World Bank.

—— (1986b) *The Development Challenges of the Eighties: A. W. Clausen at the World Bank: Major Policy Addresses, 1981–1986*, Washington DC, World Bank.

—— (1988) *Annual Report 1988*, Washington DC, World Bank.

—— (1989) *Sub-Saharan Africa: From Crisis to Sustainable Growth*, Washington DC, World Bank.

—— (1990a) *The Long-term Perspective Study of Sub-Saharan Africa*, 4 vols, Washington DC, World Bank.

—— (1990b) *How the World Bank Works with Nongovernmental Organizations*, Washington DC, World Bank.

—— (1990c) *The Conable Years at the World Bank: Major Policy Addresses*, Washington DC, World Bank.

—— (1990d), 'Freestanding Technical Assistance for Institutional Development in Sub-Saharan Africa', *OED Precis*.

—— (1991a) *World Development Report 1991*, Washington DC, World Bank.

—— (1991b) *Annual Report 1991*, Washington DC, World Bank.

—— (1992a) *Disbursement Handbook*, Washington DC, World Bank.

—— (1992b) *Governance and Development*, Washington DC, World Bank.

—— (1992c) 'Ghana 2000 and Beyond: Setting the Stage for Accelerated Growth and Poverty Reduction', West Africa Department, report number 11486-GH.

—— (1992d) 'Republic of Ghana: Literacy And Functional Skills Project', Staff Appraisal Report, report number 10164-GH.

—— (1993a) *East Asian Miracle: Economic Growth and Public Policy*, Oxford, Oxford University Press for the World Bank.

—— (1993b), 'Supply-side response to adjustment in Zambia', OED Precis, World Bank.

—— (1993c) 'Ghana – Strengthening Local Initiative And Building Local Capacity', West Africa Department, report number 11369-GH.

—— (1994a) *Governance: The World Bank's Experience*, Washington DC, World Bank.

—— (1994b) *Evaluation Results 1992*, Operations Evaluation Department, Washington DC, World Bank.

—— (1994c) 'World Bank sourcebook on participation', Environmentally Sustainable Development, Draft.

—— (1994d) 'Republic of Ghana: Local Government Development Project', Staff Appraisal Report, report number 12332-GH.

—— (1994e) 'Ghana: Community Water And Sanitation Project', Staff Appraisal Report, report number 12404-GH.

—— (1995a) *Evaluation Results 1993*, Operations Evaluation Department, Washington DC, World Bank.

—— (1995b) 'Ghana: Country Assistance Review' Operations Evaluation Department, Washington DC, World Bank.

—— (1995c) 'Cooperation between the World Bank and NGOs: FY 1994 progress report', World Bank paper.

—— (1995d) 'The World Bank and legal technical assistance: initial lessons', Policy Research Working Paper, Legal Department, World Bank.

—— (1995e) 'Technical Annex: The Republic of Ghana: Non-Bank Financial Institutions Assistance Project', West Central Africa Department, report number T-6696-GH.

—— (1996a) 'Technical Annex: The Republic of Ghana: Public Enterprise And Privatization Technical Assistance Project', West Central Africa Department, report number T-6901-GH.

—— (1996b) 'Technical Annex: Republic of Ghana: Public Financial Management Technical Assistance Project', West Central Africa Department, report number T-6977-GH.

—— (1998a) *World Development Report 1998*, Washington DC, World Bank.

—— (1998b) *Assessing Aid: What Works, What Doesn't and Why*, Oxford, Oxford University Press for the World Bank.

—— (1999a) *World Development Report 1998/1999*, Washington DC, World Bank.

—— (1999b) *Knowledge Management*, Washington DC, World Bank.

—— (1999c) 'Public Sector Management Reform Project', Africa Region, Project Appraisal Document, report no. 19004-GH.

—— (2000a) 'Monitoring and Evaluation Capacities in Ghana – A Diagnosis And Proposed Action Plan', World Bank paper.

World Bank (2000b) 'Ghana: Country Assistance Evaluation', Operations Evaluation Department, report No. 20328.

—— (2000c) 'Public Financial Management Reform Project', Africa Region, report no. PID9535.

—— (2002a) *A Sourcebook for Poverty Reduction Strategies*, Washington DC, World Bank.

—— (2002b) 'Non-Bank Financial Institutions Assistance Project: Implementation Completion Report', report no. 25213.

—— (2002c) 'Second Community Water And Sanitation Project: Implementation Completion Report', report no. 32309, 9 June 2005.

—— (2003a) 'Republic of Ghana: Poverty Reduction Support Credit and Grant: Program Document', Africa Region, report no. 25995-GH.

—— (2003b) 'Local Government Development Project: Implementation Completion Report', report no. 27064.

—— (2003c) 'Land Administration Project', Africa Regional Office, Project Appraisal Document, report no. 25913.

World Bank (2003d) 'Promoting Partnerships with Traditional Authorities Project', Africa Regional Office, Project Appraisal Document, report no. 25155-GH.

—— (2004a) *Books, Buildings and Learning Outcomes: An Impact Evaluation of World Bank Support to Basic Education in Ghana*, Operations Evaluation Department, Washington DC, World Bank.

—— (2004b) 'Country Assistance Strategy of the World Bank Group for the Republic of Ghana', 20 February 2004, African Region, report no. 27838-GH.

—— (2004c) 'Public Financial Management Technical Assistance Project: Implementation Completion Report', report no. 28089-GH.

—— (2004d) 'Community-Based Rural Development Project', Project Appraisal Document, report no. 28539.

—— (2004e) 'Public Sector Management Reform Project: Implementation Completion Report', report no. 2751-GH.

—— (2005a) *Evaluation Results 2004*, Washington DC, World Bank.

—— (2005b) *Capacity Building in Africa: An OED Evaluation of World Bank Support*, Operations Evaluation Department, Washington DC, World Bank.

—— (2005c) 'An Independent Review of World Bank Support to Capacity Building in Africa: The Case of Ghana', Operations Evaluation Department, World Bank.

—— (2005d) 'Implementation Completion Report: Second Community Water and Sanitation Project', report no. 32309.

—— (2005e) 'Micro, Small and Medium Enterprises Project', Africa Region, Project Appraisal Document, report no. 31985-GH.

—— (2005f) 'Public Enterprise and Privatization Report', Technical Assistance Project: Implementation Completion Report, report no. 32669.

Young, T. (1995) '"A project to be realised": global liberalism and contemporary Africa', *Millennium* 24, 3: 527–46.

Zacher, M. (1991) 'The decaying pillars of the Westphalian temple', in Rosenau, J. and Czempiel, E. (eds), *Governance Without Government: Order and Change in World Politics*, Cambridge, Cambridge University Press.

Zastoupil, L. (1994) *John Stuart Mill and India*, Stanford, Stanford University Press.

Index

Printed in the United States
by Baker & Taylor Publisher Services